Chelsea Today

A striking new photographic portrait of Chelsea.

Chelsea – the fashionable village in London covering ᴜᴜ acres – is one of the liveliest and most popular parts of the capital.

Roger George Clark's pictures and words capture the essence of this fast-changing area, highlighting landmarks such as Wren's Royal Hospital and King's Road, and exploring the secret places, hidden gardens and bohemian streetlife.

A dazzling array of characters crowd the pages – royalty, spies, statesmen, traitors, artists, writers, musicians and stage and screen stars; from Oscar Wilde to Augustus John, Mozart, Tolstoy, Mrs Simpson, Kim Philby, Lord Haw-Haw, Margaret Thatcher, Judy Garland, and Laurence Olivier and Vivien Leigh. Roger George Clark tracks down the places where the famous and infamous lived. And the cafés, antique shops, boutiques and pubs that make up Chelsea's unique character are explored and documented in over 100 photographs.

Roger George Clark has known Chelsea since childhood. He has taken photographs for more than twenty years. His pictures are in the National Portrait Gallery and have been exhibited at the National Theatre. His previous book *Henley: the regatta* (with Daniel Topolski) was warmly received. He works full-time as a BBC producer and broadcaster and spent two years on the editorial staff of the *Observer* after starting his career in publishing.

Overleaf: F. Derwent Wood's statue of Atlanta on the Chelsea Embankment near the Albert Bridge.

Chelsea Today

ROGER GEORGE CLARK

ROBERT HALE · LONDON

ISBN 0 7090 4427 5

Robert Hale Limited
Clerkenwell House
Clerkenwell Green
London EC1R 0HT

Map by Edanart

Photoset in North Wales by
Derek Doyle & Associates, Mold, Clwyd.
Printed and bound in Hong Kong by
Bookbuilders Ltd.

Contents

To Nic Newman

Burton's Court with the Royal Hospital behind.

Stone guardians in Old Church Street, the most ancient street in Chelsea.

Shoppers scurry along King's Road on a damp Saturday afternoon.

The delicately strutted Albert Bridge links Chelsea to Battersea.

Acknowledgements

I would like to thank John le Carré for clarifying details about George Smiley's 'home' in Chelsea, Sir Peter Hall for information about rehearsals in Petyt House and Ursula Vaughan Williams for telling me about her husband, the composer, who spent twenty-four years in Cheyne Walk. Angela Douglas kindly told me about her husband Kenneth More and his connection with Sir Thomas More.

Col. Henry Townend gave me a warm welcome at Hill House School. So did Julian Humphrys at the National Army Museum. Mr J.E. Carruthers smoothed my path at the Royal Hospital and gave valuable advice.

I would like to thank the Marquis of Normanby, Richard Rogers and Julian Barrow for permission to photograph their homes, and Martin Summers who allowed me to photograph his roof garden. The Artistic Director of the Royal Court Theatre, Max Stafford-Clark, let me eavesdrop on a rehearsal. The rectors of Chelsea Old Church, St Luke's and Holy Trinity were good enough to allow cameras in their churches as were the owners of Crosby Hall and the National Trust, which owns Carlyle's house.

And my thanks to Ann Kaye for her help, and to the staff of Chelsea Public Library, who were always willing to answer a query and search their files at the drop of a hat.

Charles II, founder of the Royal Hospital.

Chelsea Studios, created 1925–30 as a place of beauty for artists to work.
It resembles a Tuscan village near Florence, but lies near Chelsea
Football Ground. Vines and walnut trees came from Italy.

Outdoor cafés in Chelsea Farmers Market, Sydney Street. On this site in 1685 the King's gardener grew plants and herbs to adorn the Palace of Westminster.

1   The Bohemian Square Mile

Two hundred yards from the busy King's Road stands a house with a green door. It's in a quiet terrace where crowds seldom go, opposite Sir Christopher Wren's Royal Hospital. Here lived the creator of one of the most sinister figures in modern literature. As you crunch your way over the gravel forecourt and peer over black iron railings a blue plaque on the wall proclaims: 'Bram Stoker (1847–1912) author of *Dracula* lived here.'

Dracula in Chelsea? It's curious to find this evil figure commemorated in a London street. But national and international personalities, notorious and eminent, saturate Chelsea's history. Oscar Wilde wrote his plays and crashed in ruin here. Britain's first prime minister, Sir Robert Walpole, and first woman prime minister, Margaret Thatcher, made it their home. So did David Lloyd George who led the country to victory in the First World War.

The Prince of Wales went to school in Chelsea. His future wife, Lady Diana Spencer, spent a year in the district before marrying into the royal family. Fictional spies James Bond and George Smiley 'lived' in Chelsea. Real spies stalk the streets. 'This is the spies' church you know,' said the verger of one fashionable house of prayer. 'The lady who does the flowers was in naval intelligence and the former head of MI5 comes here to worship.' Donald Maclean, who defected to the USSR with Guy Burgess, was a Chelsea resident as was the British agent, Greville Wynne. And one of the most successful spies in history, the KGB double agent, Kim Philby, leased a house in Carlyle Square where his mistress ran a nursery school.

In the summer of 1955 the *Daily Telegraph* reported 'Strange Happenings in Chelsea'. Cheyne Row was crowded with hansom cabs, trotting horses, a fire-engine belching smoke and people in Victorian dress, while a Mexican comedian rode up and down on a penny-farthing bicycle. Film makers were at work on *Around the World in Eighty Days*.

18 St Leonard's Terrace, home of the author of Dracula.

Denims and bleached hair, the punk look King's Road.

Madonna look-alike, King's Road.

The miniskirt was invented in Chelsea, *Rule Britannia* composed in King's Road, *Winnie-the-Pooh* written close by. Britain's most famous actor, Laurence Olivier, lived at various addresses in or near Chelsea from the 1930s until his death in 1989. Mick Jagger and Keith Richard of the Rolling Stones found themselves expensive houses on the embankment. The poet Dylan Thomas said he 'hated' the area and, like Karl Marx a century before, suffered in poverty further inland, while the Hollywood star Judy Garland ended her life with an overdose of sleeping tablets in a mews cottage.

Chelsea boasts at least one saint (Sir Thomas More) and three traitors. Besides Maclean and Philby it was the home of Lord Haw-Haw. Like Sir Thomas, he died on the scaffold.

Chelsea contains a building where Richard III plotted his way to the throne, the tomb of the man whose antiquities helped found the British Museum, the oldest rock garden in Europe (it's listed), and a street named after one of the killers of Charles I. The novelist, Charles Dickens, married in Chelsea as did the woman who provoked the greatest royal scandal in the twentieth century, Mrs Simpson, later Duchess of Windsor.

In Chelsea you can find Napoleon's horse, the hastily scribbled order that started the charge of the Light Brigade, Mark Twain's application for tickets at the local library, Scott of the Antarctic's home, and the most expensive hotel suite in London – £2,000 a night – and that excludes breakfast.

The Russian novelist Leo Tolstoy, coaxed essays out of local school children in 1861. His visit lasted only a day, but other writers have longer associations. The essayists Addison and Steele lived here at the beginning of the eighteenth century, as did the satirist and author of *Gulliver's Travels*, Jonathan Swift. Leigh Hunt dwelt in squalor with his large family round the corner from Thomas Carlyle, who spent forty-seven years in the neighbourhood. George Eliot died after only three weeks in Chelsea, and Henry James passed away in a flat overlooking the river. It was the home of the Scottish novelist, Tobias Smollett, also of Jane Austen, Katherine Mansfield, Arnold Bennett, Hilaire Belloc, Radclyffe Hall (whose lesbian novel *The Well of Loneliness* caused outrage in 1928 and was banned), Peter and Ian Fleming, and the Poet Laureate, Sir John Betjeman.

Mozart played music in Ranelagh Gardens when a child, and Ralph Vaughan Williams composed some of his finest works during the twenty-four years he lived in Cheyne Walk. And if you ventured past Osbert Sitwell's home in Carlyle Square one winter's day in 1922, you could have heard the first

Chelsea Old Church, bombed in 1941, but reconstructed exactly as it was.

Statue of Sir Thomas More outside the Old Church where he worshipped and sang in the choir.

Imaginative displays by over 700 exhibitors attract 250,000 visitors to Chelsea Flower Show each summer.

Champagne, caviare, smoked salmon and modest fare are served to visitors who come to the five-day show from all over the world.

The world's largest tent, the Great Marquee, covers 3½ acres of the
Royal Hospital Grounds. Ranelagh Pleasure Gardens occupied the site
in the eighteenth century.

performance of Edith Sitwell's and William Walton's *Façade* floating out of the windows of the first floor drawing-room.

Then there are the artists. Holbein painted Sir Thomas More and his family in their Chelsea mansion in the 1620s. Three centuries later, the great landscape and seascape painter Turner, whose work is displayed in a special gallery at the Tate a couple of miles downstream, lived his last years in a cottage overlooking the river. The Pre-Raphaelites followed – Dante Gabriel Rossetti, William and Jane Morris, Holman Hunt, Swinburne, Millais, while Whistler, Sargent, Epstein, Augustus John, Orpen and Sickert savoured the informal atmosphere. And a future emperor of Japan sat for his portrait in a Chelsea studio.

Chelsea's architecture is mostly domestic, though Sir Christopher Wren graced the borough with one of his grandest buildings – the Royal Hospital. Each year the bleakest parts of the hospital's grounds are transformed into the world's greatest flower show. In the 1980s the controversial architect, Richard Rogers, gutted two Regency houses nearby and constructed one of the most daring domestic interiors in London.

Today most artists have gone – driven out by high rents and high prices. 'Mayfair has come to Chelsea,' said one disconsolate resident. Film makers, pop musicians, designers, cartoonists, television and show business personalities, antique dealers and millionaires have moved in to take their place. The actor Michael Caine owns a penthouse in Chelsea Harbour, where Patrick Lichfield and Viscount Linley run a stylish restaurant. King's Road, heart of 'Swinging London' in the 1960s, still swings. On Saturday afternoons the inhabitants of *Vogue, Tatler, Arena, ID, GQ* and other trend-setting magazines parade along its pavements and swarm into pubs, clubs, cafés and boutiques.

Chelsea, although linked administratively to Kensington since 1965, still retains its distinctive character. Officially it is bounded by the Fulham and Brompton Roads, the Thames and Westminster – a fashionable triangle a mile-and-a-half long, covering 660 acres. Yet Chelsea has always had elastic boundaries. Neighbours in less desirable areas along its borders claim it as their own. But Chelsea Barracks, Chelsea Football Club, Chelsea Harbour, Chelsea Studios and half Chelsea Bridge lie outside the borough, as does Chelsea Gardens, the block of flats where Jerome K. Jerome wrote *Three Men in a Boat*. So frontiers are less clear-cut than those drawn on a map.

Artist Julian Barrow's studio in Tite Street.

2   A Village of Palaces

The origin of the name 'Chelsea', which is spelt in at least thirty ways, is disputed. One theory suggests it could mean 'chalk wharf'. A wharf stood here from early times and traces of chalk were spotted at low tide. Authorities also differ about the foundation of Chelsea Old Church which, until its destruction in the Second World War, was Chelsea's oldest building. Some say the church dated from pre-Norman or possibly Saxon times. Documentary evidence tells us a church was here in 1157. Cottages sprang up round it and isolated farms appeared in the countryside, but Chelsea remained a small village until the eighteenth century.

Chelsea's oldest building now is a transplant. Crosby Hall, near Battersea Bridge, originally stood over four miles away in Bishopsgate. It was part of a large medieval mansion, Crosby Place, but in 1910 it was moved stone by stone to Chelsea. The site in Bishopsgate was bought by a bank and the only way to save the hall was to take it down and re-erect it elsewhere. The hall was built in 1466 by a wealthy merchant and member of parliament, Sir John Crosby. On his death his widow let the building to Richard, Duke of Gloucester. It was his London residence before he seized the throne as Richard III. When you enter the hall today you see it much as Richard did – a magnificent oak and chestnut roof decorated in gold, scarlet and green. Doubtless he would recognize the delicately vaulted oriel window with Sir John's crest on the roof.

Crosby Place is mentioned in Shakespeare's *Richard III*. Over the centuries the hall passed through many hands. At one time it was the headquarters of the East India Company. Then it became a scientific and literary institute, a post office, a church and a restaurant. From 1862–7 it was a wine merchants and Mr Gladstone's favourite claret was stored in the chimney.

During rebuilding in Chelsea something was lost – a feeling of age. The hall might be Gothic revival, rather than genuinely medieval, such is the perfection of its reconstruction.

Richard III's and Sir Thomas More's Crosby Hall.

By a remarkable coincidence the building rose again on what was once part of Sir Thomas More's Chelsea garden. The Tudor statesman had owned the hall in Bishopsgate and used it for entertaining while he was Henry VIII's Lord Chancellor. But from 1524 he and his large family moved to a country mansion (later Beaufort House) in Chelsea, west of the church.

More was in his forties when he came to Chelsea, where he spent the rest of his life. This epitome of Renaissance man, friend of scholars and author of *Utopia*, had trained as a lawyer and become a member of parliament. Introduced to Henry VIII by Cardinal Wolsey, he rose rapidly in the King's favour, was made speaker of the House of Commons and sent on missions abroad to Francis I and Charles V. When Wolsey fell in 1529 he became Lord Chancellor.

Erasmus, a personal friend for over thirty-five years, described More's home as 'not mean, nor invidiously grand, but comfortable'. It was set in acres of gardens and orchards, which stretched from the river to King's Road. The house was close to the city, court and parliament at Westminster, to which Sir Thomas travelled on horseback, or in a barge rowed by eight watermen.

For many years More remained high in Henry's esteem. The King was a frequent visitor to Chelsea, on one occasion arriving unannounced for dinner. Afterwards More's son-in-law, William Roper, watched as they strolled in the gardens, Henry with his arm affectionately round his chancellor's neck. Roper commented on the King's regard, but More had few illusions: 'I have no cause to be proud thereof,' he remarked, 'for if my head would win him a castle in France, it would not fail to go.'

The break came in 1532 when Henry declared himself head of the Church in England. More resigned the chancellorship in protest and returned to Chelsea. He also disapproved of the King divorcing Catherine of Aragon and marrying Anne Boleyn. The King accused him of high treason and More was imprisoned for a year in the Tower of London and beheaded in 1535. More's property was confiscated and his family turned out.

Beaufort House was pulled down 200 years later and Beaufort Street, which runs south to Battersea Bridge, built on the site. More's stableyard, however, still exists. It is now the Moravian burial ground and a small church was built on the original foundations of the stables. The chapel where More worshipped in Chelsea Old Church still stands; the church contains a long epitaph which More composed himself and the

Tomb of Sir Hans Sloane, Chelsea Old Church. Sir Hans was Lord of the Manor and his names occur all over the borough.

The graveyard, Chelsea Old Church.

graves of his two wives. Outside is a modern statue of More, his head turned slightly down river in the direction of his last journey. Each July hundreds of people re-enact this sombre occasion, sailing from Cadogan Pier to the Tower. They visit the cell where he was imprisoned, the place of execution and other sites associated with the man who was canonized 400 years after his death.

Henry was unsentimental about More's passing. A short time later he built himself a manor house overlooking the river at Chelsea where the houses numbered from 19–26 Cheyne Walk stand today. He presented the building as a wedding gift to his sixth wife, Catherine Parr, who retired there when he died in 1547.

The manor house was soon enveloped in scandal. Catherine's former lover, the Lord High Admiral Thomas Seymour, was seen visiting her early in the morning. Within four months of Henry's death they married. The young Princess Elizabeth (later Elizabeth I) was put in Catherine's charge. Then rumours began to fly. Seymour, it was alleged, was sexually harassing the princess and romping in her bedroom. Elizabeth was sent away from Chelsea and eventually Seymour was accused of a mass of offences and beheaded for high treason.

Later the manor house, which was also the home of Lady Jane Grey and Henry's fourth wife, Anne of Cleves, was occupied by Lord Howard of Effingham, who commanded the fleet that defeated the Spanish Armada. Within 200 years, however, the building was demolished, though traces of Tudor brickwork still exist.

Today, if you walk under the archway at Number 24 and down the countrified Cheyne Mews overhung by trees and greenery to the cottages at the far end, you can find part of the garden wall that belonged to the manor. A plaque at the entrance to the mews tells you: 'The old manor house garden still lies beyond the end wall of Cheyne Mews and contains mulberry trees said to have been planted by Queen Elizabeth I.' Close by two more signs warn: 'This road is reserved for residents and their horses and vehicles,' and 'All drivers of vehicles are directed to walk their horses while passing under this archway.'

The seventeenth century saw the construction of great houses – almost palaces – in Chelsea. One was built in 1623 for the courtier and parliamentarian, Sir John Danvers. He was one of the men who signed Charles I's death-warrant. Danvers

House adjoined the home of Sir Thomas More and the diarist Samuel Pepys reckoned it was 'the prettiest contrived house I ever saw in my life'. The garden, the first in England created in a formal Italian style, featured sculpture, a grotto and a bowling green. Like Sir Thomas More's estate Sir John's extended from the Thames to King's Road and his garden was on the site of Paultons Square.

Danvers is said to have repented his part in the king's execution and escaped the retribution that befell other regicides as he died in 1655, before the Restoration. When his house was pulled down in the next century the driveway was transformed into the street that now bears his name. Number 20a has a blue plaque for it was here that the bacteriologist Sir Alexander Fleming lived. In 1928 he discovered the first antibiotic, penicillin. The travel writer Peter Fleming lived directly above in flat Number 20, a source of confusion for postmen as they were unrelated.

After Charles II came to the throne in 1660 Chelsea became fashionable, patronized by the King and his court. The only large mansion that remains from this period when Chelsea was called 'a village of palaces' is Lindsey House, on the embankment near Battersea Bridge. In the eighteenth century the building was divided into separate houses that lie behind a high wall and eagle-topped gateway.

Chelsea is mentioned in the diaries of John Evelyn and Samuel Pepys, the latter visiting the Old Church in March 1663 'expecting to see the young ladies of the schoole' and failing and then, a few weeks before the Great Fire that destroyed much of London in 1666, walking home across the fields from the Swan Tavern at Chelsea 'it being a mighty fine, cool evening'. The tavern was on the water's edge at the bottom of the present Swan Walk. A few months earlier Pepys had fled from the same spot for fear of the plague: ' ... a gentleman walking by called to us that the house was shut up of the sickness. So with great affright turned back ... and went away (I for my part in great disorder) for Kensington; and there I spent about 30s upon the jades with great pleasure ... '

The end of the seventeenth century was marked by two notable events in Chelsea – the founding of the Physic Garden and the building of Wren's Royal Hospital.

The Physic Garden was created in 1673 by the Society of Apothecaries for the study of plants used in medicine. The garden, second oldest in England after Oxford, covers three-and-a-half acres, and before the embankment was built

The Physic Garden, Swan Walk, was established in 1673. The first cedar trees to grow in England were planted here. The garden contains the largest olive tree in Britain and one of the oldest rock gardens.

The garden's saviour,
Sir Hans Sloane.

The Apothecaries Society's coat of
arms showing Apollo slaying the
dragon of disease.

ran down to the river close to the Swan tavern. When the garden was founded plants were the major source of medicine; here apothecaries and physicians learnt how to recognize and use them. John Evelyn, who was a member of the Royal Society, came to see the first gardener, John Watts, in the summer of 1685 and was impressed by the 'ingenious and subterranean heate, conveyed by a stove under the conservatory, which was all vaulted with brick, so as he leaves the doores and windows open in the hardest frosts ... '

Half a century later the garden was in financial difficulties, but was saved by the Lord of the Manor, Sir Hans Sloane, who had studied botany there in his youth, and now owned the lease. He presented this to the Apothecaries Society on condition the botanic garden was preserved and 2,000 plants given to the Royal Society at the rate of fifty a year. Sir Hans's generosity is commemorated by a white marble statue carved by John Rysbrack, a copy of which stands in the centre of the grounds. The original, blurred and pitted by time, was removed to the British Museum to preserve what was left.

The garden claims to have the oldest rock garden in Europe. This was constructed from blocks of lava brought back from Iceland in 1772 by Sir Joseph Banks, the English botanist who sailed round the world with Captain Cook. The rock garden also contains building stones from the Tower of London and is listed as an historic monument.

The Physic Garden has been described as 'a living library' for botanic research. Plants are exchanged with countries all over the world and it was from here that cotton seed was sent to the United States to help found their cotton plantations.

Today the garden is no longer in the country. Houses and flats crowd in on three sides, but these shelter the grounds from winds and radiate heat in winter, providing a benign climate in which exotic trees, shrubs and vegetation can flourish. Rare birds and insects flit among the plants and shaded walks, and ancient trees droop over flowerbeds. Despite a devastating storm in 1987, the atmosphere of an old English garden is preserved.

Chelsea's most distinguished building, the Royal Hospital for retired soldiers, was designed by Sir Christopher Wren. It took ten years to erect. A Latin inscription in the main courtyard summarizes its construction: 'This hospital was founded by Charles II, expanded by James II and completed by King William and Queen Mary – 1692.'

Some 450 old soldiers live here, men of good character who

Chelsea pensioners gather for the Oak Apple Day parade (29 May)
when they celebrate Charles II's founding of the Royal Hospital.

are at least 65 and 'broken by war or old age'. On entering the hospital they give up their pensions in return for board, lodging, clothing and medical care. The average age is 76.

Charles II's building was inspired by Louis XIV's Les Invalides in Paris. He discussed plans with the Paymaster-General of the Army, Sir Stephen Fox, who organized the finances, and John Evelyn. The King's Surveyor-General, Sir Christopher Wren, chose the site of a ruined theological college in Chelsea and drew up plans for a vast building – a palace for veterans. 'The work of a gentleman' said Thomas Carlyle and you can see what he meant if you look behind the screen of trees in Royal Hospital Road and examine that endless, but carefully articulated façade – polite, unemphatic and a trifle forbidding. No raised voices here, except on parade. Wren chose red brick and Portland stone, set Doric porticoes, crowned by a lantern, at the focal point and decorated the skyline with massive chimneys. It was the architect's first large-scale secular work and a model for future official buildings on both sides of the Atlantic. 'Wren's masterpiece', remarked Sir John Betjeman on one occasion, forgetting St Paul's.

Wren refused to design purely for show. As a practical architect he appreciated the problems of old age. He devised shallow steps to make stairs easy to climb and constructed a colonnade where pensioners could enjoy fresh air sheltered from sun, wind and rain. Oak cabins with doors for privacy were built in the long wards. In the chapel the pulpit and reading desk were placed half way down amid the congregation to help the hard of hearing.

The hospital is similar to an Oxford College. Buildings are grouped round courtyards. The most imposing, Figure Court, is named after Grinling Gibbons's bronze figure of Charles II that stands in the centre. The statue faces the great hall and chapel that lie on either side of an octagonal entrance hall, adorned with staves and trophies captured in battle. Pensioners take their meals in the great hall where, in 1852, the body of the Duke of Wellington lay in state for a week.

The men who live in the hospital today are divided into six companies with a Governor and officers in charge. They still wear eighteenth-century uniforms – blue in winter, scarlet in summer – with three-cornered hats for special occasions.

Grinling Gibbons's statue of Charles II in Roman uniform stands in Figure Court, the oldest part of Sir Christopher Wren's Royal Hospital.

3 Gardens of Delight

By the end of Charles II's reign Chelsea was still a quiet country village with about a thousand inhabitants and forty baptisms a year. King's Road was the monarch's private thoroughfare used on his way to Hampton Court. It remained private until 1830 and others could use it only if they held a copper pass stamped 'The King's Private Roads'.

A contemporary account in 1694 noted 'the number of houses are mightily increased of late years, for there are 350 houses in the parish'. Chelsea was changing, Tudor mansions disappearing and smaller houses taking their place. The Cheyne family, who were Lords of the Manor of Chelsea from 1660 to 1712, gave their name to Cheyne Row and Cheyne Walk, where building began, as well as Cheyne Mews, Place and Row.

Meanwhile, the satirist Jonathan Swift made his home in Church Lane, where Crosby Hall now stands. Swift was in his forties and had yet to write *Gulliver's Travels*. He makes frequent references to Chelsea in his *Journal to Stella* where he sometimes cuts a comic figure. One summer he described splashing about in the Thames with his landlady's napkin on his head, while his servant waited for him to come ashore. Swift had swum for half an hour and dived beneath the waters ' … but as I dived, the napkin fell off and is lost, and I have that to pay for … ' A short time later he staggered to the bank, 'O faith, the great stones were so sharp, I could hardly set my feet on them as I came out.'

About the same time in 1712 the manor was bought by the royal physician and later President of the Royal Society, Sir Hans Sloane. His name appears all over Chelsea, most prominently in Sloane Square and Sloane Street – not to mention Sloane Rangers. His first name also turns up in Hans Town, Crescent, Place, Road, Street and elsewhere. Sloane was a formidable collector. His museum and library of 50,000 books

The eighteenth-century house in Cheyne Walk where George Eliot died in 1880.

and manuscripts formed the nucleus of the British Museum. When he died in his 90s in 1753 he was buried at Chelsea Old Church. His estate was divided between his two daughters the youngest of whom, Lady Cadogan, was specially favoured. Ninety-four acres of Chelsea are still owned by the Cadogan family, including 4,000 flats, 700 houses, 300 shops and stores and numerous offices.

They were to come later, but by the middle of the eighteenth century a foreign visitor noted: 'On all sides round about Chelsea there is scarcely seen anything else than either orchards or vegetable market gardens, and beautiful houses as it were scattered amongst them ... The place resembles a town, has a church, beautiful streets, well built and handsome houses of brick, three or four stories high ... '

The Old Rectory, a notable survival from the period, was built about 1725. Standing in Old Church Street, near King's Road, it is one of the few surviving Georgian rectories in London. A gateway leads to a forecourt, coach house and cobbled yard and the building has one of the largest private gardens in London, after Buckingham Palace. This covers two-and-a-quarter acres and is walled on all sides. The Duke of Wellington's brother, the Rev Gerald Valerian Wellesley, occupied the rectory and the duke enjoyed sitting in the garden beneath the shade of an old mulberry tree, reputedly planted by Elizabeth I.

The house has a blue plaque for the author Charles Kingsley lived here when his father was rector. Charles was a combative religious socialist, a vigorous exponent of muscular Christianity. He lived in the rectory for only two years though, long before he won fame by writing *Westward Ho!* and *The Water Babies*.

Chelsea became a centre for entertainment in 1742 when Ranelagh Gardens opened close to the Royal Hospital. They were named after Lord Ranelagh, the Paymaster-General of the Forces and Treasurer of the hospital, who built a large house on the eastern side and laid out an extensive park.

After his death the estate was bought by a syndicate and transformed into a pleasure garden. At its centre was the Rotunda, a huge circular wooden building, larger than the Pantheon in Rome. 'There is a vast amphitheatre,' enthused Horace Walpole, 'finely gilt, painted, and illuminated, into which everybody that loves eating, drinking, staring, or crowding, is admitted for 12 pence.' Nearby was an ornamental lake and canal on which a Chinese pavilion appeared to float.

Tourists relax on the rim of the Venus fountain, Sloane Square.

At night these gardens were brilliantly illuminated said Smollett 'with a thousand golden lamps that emulate the noon-day sun'. Royalty and high society flocked to masquerades, banquets, balls, regattas, fireworks and musical entertainments. Women of fashion glided among the trees 'swimming by you like swans' observed one old gentleman. Dr Johnson gave his approval, Canaletto painted the Rotunda and concerts were organized by the leading theatrical musician, Thomas Arne, who lived at 215 King's Road and composed *Rule Britannia*.

An advertisement appeared in 1764 promising 'the most extraordinary Prodigy, the most amazing Genius that has appeared in any Age'. This hyperbole had substance. 'In the Course of the Evening's Entertainments the celebrated and astonishing Master MOZART, lately arrived, a Child of 7 years of Age, will perform several select Pieces of his own Composition on the Harpsichord and on the Organ ... ' Mozart's real age was 8½, but few disputed his ability. Indeed he wrote his first symphony in a house a few hundred yards away, Number 180 Ebury Street.

Ranelagh's popularity helped sales of Chelsea buns that were made close by in Pimlico Road. The buns, which were square, were full of butter, sugar, lemon and spice. The Chelsea Bun House was decorated with clocks, statues and antiques, and patronized by royalty. George II and Queen Caroline and George III and Queen Charlotte and the princesses were all customers. On Good Fridays thousands gathered for Hot Cross Buns. By 1793 there were so many people that the proprietor, Mrs Hand, feared a riot and closed the shop over Easter.

The Chelsea Bun House stayed in business for 150 years, but closed in 1839 after a quarter of a million buns were sold on Good Friday. Ranelagh had disappeared 30 years before as people of fashion deserted the area and this affected the Bun House as well. The Rotunda was pulled down, the canal vanished and today there is no trace of one of London's most glamorous pleasure grounds. A simple brick summer-house by Sir John Soane marks the site of the Rotunda in a landscaped garden. Chelsea pensioners stroll along the paths feeding grey squirrels that scamper among bushes and up trees, while children gambol on lawns with their parents and nannies. But come May and magic returns. For a week Ranelagh and the adjoining South Grounds are transformed into the Chelsea Flower Show.

Sloane Street and Sloane Square were laid out towards the

end of the eighteenth century and the architect, Henry Holland, built Hans Town in the north. Bollards marking the boundary of the new town still exist, including one outside the Danish Embassy in Sloane Street. The novelist, Jane Austen, stayed with her brother at 23 Hans Place. The house has since disappeared, but its site is marked by a plaque.

'About the year 1796,' wrote Thomas Faulkner in his local history, 'I was present at a staghunt in Chelsea. The animal swam across the river from Battersea, and made for Lord Cremorne's grounds. Upon being driven from thence, he ran along the water-side as far as the church, and turning up Church Lane, at last took refuge in Mrs Hutchin's barn, where he was taken alive.'

At the turn of the nineteenth century large tracts of land were still country gardens supplying vegetables and fruit for London. The Duke of York's school for soldiers' orphans, now a territorial army headquarters, opened in King's Road near Sloane Square in 1801. About this time 12,000 people lived in Chelsea. Terraces of brick houses went up near the Old Church and Cheyne Walk and Cheyne Row filled up. The increasing number of people put pressure on the church that could hold a congregation of only 450. It was also too far away from the most densely populated part of the parish. So a new church, St Luke's, was built in 1824 near the centre of Chelsea in Sydney Street. Twenty-nine architects, including Sir John Soane and John Nash, submitted plans, but James Savage's design was chosen. Savage went back to the past, to Gothic architecture, with stone vaults and flying buttresses, and a tower 142 feet high. He created a small cathedral. The east end of St Luke's resembled King's College chapel, Cambridge, but Savage was more sparing in his detail. His design has provoked critics ever since. The church was a 'fraud' maintained Ian Nairn, 'one of the most loveless in London ... ' Nikolaus Pevsner thought its proportions 'lanky' and the detail 'papery'. Kenneth Clark took a more balanced view in his book *The Gothick Revival*. There was 'something distinguished in its slim tower,' he mused, something 'almost exciting in its perverse flying buttresses'. But he admitted the construction was meagre and looked cardboard. John Betjeman thought it 'great architecture'.

Charles Dickens married in St Luke's on 2 April, 1836. The wedding was quiet, with only the family present. The bride, Catherine Hogarth, was the daughter of the editor of the *Evening Chronicle* where Dickens' 'Sketches of Boz' appeared. Catherine lived nearby and the wedding took place shortly

St Luke's, Sydney Street, designed by James Savage, was one of the first medieval revival buildings in Britain. John Betjeman admired its 'paper-thin Georgian Gothic'.

St Luke's interior. When built in 1824 this was the loftiest nave in London after Westminster Abbey and St Paul's. Novelist Charles Dickens was married here in 1836.

after the first part of *Pickwick Papers* was published. The marriage, however, was unhappy. Twenty-two years later after she had borne him ten children, Catherine and her husband separated. No two people 'had less in common', wrote Dickens bitterly.

Half a mile away from St Luke's, at the western end of Chelsea near the river, lay Cremorne Gardens. They had opened with a sports stadium, but gardens similar to Ranelagh developed later and attracted the working classes. Stunts brought in the crowds. Madame Geneviève teetered across the Thames on a tightrope and 500 soldiers stormed a fort, the stage collapsing beneath them.

Cremorne Gardens are best remembered for aerial dramas. In 1839 Mr Hampton sailed two miles up in a balloon and descended by parachute. Charles Green, 'the intrepid aviator', went aloft with a leopard and a lady and, in 1852, a woman wearing a scarlet cloak rode side-saddle on the back of a violently kicking bull hoisted into the air. A monster balloon, nearly 100 feet in diameter, which was tethered to the ground by a rope 2,000 feet long, one day broke loose, soared into the sky and disappeared.

Unfortunately the gardens gained a reputation for row-diness. They were a 'nursery of every kind of vice' declared a local clergyman. By 1877 the authorities had had enough. Cremorne was closed. Houses and Lots Road power-station, which supplies electricity to the Underground, replaced the gardens. There are two reminders, though, of what existed. The gates, which were at the grand entrance in King's Road, now stand in a small embankment garden. And the early aviators are commemorated by a Victorian-style pub with one of the longest names in London – 'the Ferret and Firkin in the Balloon up the Creek'. Beer is brewed on the premises and on special occasions the landlord produces a potent ale – 'Balloonatic' – which, he says, is 'very, very strong'.

By the time Cremorne Gardens closed the whole riverscape had changed. The old wooded embankment, celebrated by Thomas Rowlandson, with trees, houses and boats at the water's edge, while picturesque, was muddy and smelly at low tide. In summer the stink was unbearable. Sewage, from an increasing number of people who lived in the area, poured into the Thames. The Victorian engineer, Sir Joseph Bazalgette devised an imaginative plan. Between 1871–4 he built a sewer along the river and put a road on top. This cut off from the Thames the Old Church, the village, Cheyne Walk, the Physic Garden and Royal Hospital. Bazalgette's plan had sweep. He

Gates to the former pleasure grounds of Cremorne Gardens stand in a small park by the Thames.

Toll houses still stand at both ends of the Albert Bridge. The deck was strengthened in 1971–3 to take increased traffic and marching feet.

more than anyone transformed London's river. His embankments, including that at Chelsea, stretched for 3½ miles along the Thames. Elaborate cast-iron lamps, decorated with dolphins, adorned the grey granite walls which narrowed the river, hemmed in the tides and sped the waters so the Thames no longer froze in winter. Dickens and Carlyle were impressed. So was the young architect Hugh Casson (later President of the Royal Academy) who in the 1930s lived in Cheyne Walk overlooking the boatyards near Battersea Bridge. Bazalgette, he wrote, invested 'everything he touched, however mundane, with an engaging sagger. A great man.'

Bazalgette also demolished one of Whistler's favourite subjects, the old wooden Battersea Bridge that trembled underfoot and hindered navigation. It was built a century before by Earl Spencer, a direct ancestor of Lady Diana Spencer, who became Princess of Wales. According to the writer, William Gaunt, a legend grew up round the bridge 'that the particular confluence of airs, to be met with half-way across, possessed some strange curative and healthful magic nowhere else existing'. In its place Bazalgette designed the present bridge with five cast-iron arches.

Downstream there is grace and elegance. R.M. Ordish, who made the working drawings for the Crystal Palace, designed a Gothic suspension bridge – a fantasy in iron. He had already built something similar in Prague. Now he gave London the Albert Bridge – spiky and spindly – a gentle curve that leapt across the river, suspended by delicate struts from four towers that might adorn a fairy castle. For many years the bridge was painted dark green. This gave the structure a sinister air, an atmosphere of menace, so some critics claimed it was the ugliest in London.

For the Festival of Britain, in 1951, the Albert Bridge was brightly painted to emphasize once more its eccentric beauty. But as pedestrians crossed the river the bridge bounced up and down. Notices on toll houses at both ends warned: 'ALL TROOPS MUST BREAK STEP WHEN MARCHING OVER THIS BRIDGE'. Vibration from a thousand stamping feet might topple it into the Thames. Eventually, traffic nearly did. Continual shaking made the structure unsafe. 'Pull it down,' said the London County Council. 'No,' said John Betjeman, who protested in *The Spectator*: 'Shining with electric lights to show the way to Festival Gardens, or grey and airy against the London sky, it is one of the beauties of the London river … ' Others thought so too. The bridge was strengthened and saved.

4 Discourse Most Eloquent

Chelsea became the home of a string of writers and artists in the nineteenth century. The poet, essayist and radical, Leigh Hunt, moved to 22 Upper Cheyne Row in 1833. A gifted editor he published works by Keats, Byron, Shelley and Tennyson. By the time he came to Chelsea with his wife and seven children Hunt was fifty and impoverished. Thomas Carlyle, who acquired a house round the corner the following year, was appalled at the state of his home. It 'excels all you have ever read of – poetical Tinkerdom, without parallel even in literature'. Worse still Hunt's wife was forever borrowing from the Carlyles – spoons, tea, glasses, porridge – every form of household article – including a brass fender.

It was while visiting Leigh Hunt that Carlyle noticed a house in Cheyne Row and made inquiries. He had spent most of his life in Scotland, where he studied German literature, wrote a *Life of Schiller* and produced essays for the *Edinburgh Review*. To win success and fame he needed to move to London. Chelsea, he noted, was unfashionable and 'very dirty and confused in some places, but quite beautiful in others'. The house at 24 Cheyne Row was large and convenient and the annual running costs low. 'Goody. Rent £35,' noted Carlyle. He and his wife, Jane, moved in, accompanied by their pet canary Chico.

Carlyle began writing a major historical work, *The French Revolution*. Once the first volume was complete he lent the manuscript to the philosopher, John Stuart Mill. A few weeks later Mill arrived at Cheyne Row agitated and 'pale as Hector's ghost'. He was shown up to the first-floor library, where Carlyle had spent five months writing his history, and there broke terrible news. His maid had burnt the manuscript. She mistook it for waste paper and used it to light a fire. Nothing remained. Carlyle was stunned. Somehow this short-tempered man remained calm and determined to rewrite the work. When it and other volumes appeared the history was hailed as a masterpiece and established his reputation.

Footscraper, 2 Cheyne Row, a relic of muddy streets.

Thomas Carlyle's sitting-room, 24 Cheyne Row. Chopin played the piano and it was from a chair by the fire that Jane Carlyle sprang to welcome Leigh Hunt, inspiring his rondeau, Jenny Kissed Me.

The Sage of Chelsea, embankment gardens, Cheyne Walk. This statue of Carlyle in his dressing-gown by Sir Joseph Boehm, lies close to the author's home.

Today Carlyle is regarded more with curiosity than enthusiasm. His house, owned by the National Trust, remains much as it was when Carlyle died in his library in 1881. We can imagine him and Tennyson smoking their pipes together in the basement kitchen, see his brown felt hat on a peg by the garden door and the piano on which Chopin played in the sitting-room. Up in the attic is the desk where he wrote most of his famous works (including his *History of Frederick the Great*) and his white china inkwell with an adjustable screw to keep a uniform level of ink.

During his lifetime Carlyle was lionized. 'The Sage of Chelsea' he was called. The sculptor Sir Joseph Boehm created a striking statue for the embankment gardens. There Carlyle sits in his dressing-gown, serenely gazing over the river.

Carlyle lived for nearly half a century in Chelsea. The Russian novelist Leo Tolstoy stayed only a day. He was 32 and had yet to write *War and Peace* and *Anna Karenina*. None the less he was already well known in St Petersburg, having published a trilogy (*Childhood, Boyhood, Youth*), *Tales from Army Life* and *Sketches of Sevastopol*, based on his experiences in the Crimean War.

Tolstoy travelled through Europe and spent sixteen days in London. He watched Palmerston speaking in the House of Commons, heard Dickens give one of his famous readings and met and quarrelled with the man described as 'the greatest radical Russian thinker of the nineteenth century', Alexander Herzen, who lived in exile in Britain.

Tolstoy's visit to Chelsea was stimulated by his interest in education. The poet and critic Matthew Arnold, who was in the Department of Education, arranged for him to see the Practising School in Chelsea. This was attached to the College of St Mark where Church of England teachers trained. The Practising School provided pupils on which young teachers could try out their skills and was housed in an octagonal, yellow-brick building.

On 12 March, 1861 Tolstoy met the boys in class 3B who were aged between 10 and 14. He asked them to write descriptions of what they had done that day, how they had come to school, what games they played and what they studied in class. Their essays are the authentic voices of Victorian working-class schoolboys in Chelsea. 'Dear Sir,' wrote 12-year-old Chalkley, 'When I came to school I played at marbles and lost all mine.' Another accidentally splashed a friend who forced him to stand in a puddle until his boots were soaked. The boys came from as

Tolstoy was here. The Russian novelist visited the St Mark's Practising School on 12 March 1861. Essays he asked the pupils to write still exist.

far as five miles away. One described how he paid a toll to cross the old wooden Battersea Bridge, while another travelled downstream from Putney in a boat that 'stuck fast in the mud, for the tide was low' and had to be rescued. They studied scripture, arithmetic and Latin and, besides marbles, played cricket and spun wooden tops. It was wet, 'very showery' and there was hail.

The novelist took these essays back to Russia where they are preserved in the Tolstoy Museum in Moscow.

Tolstoy's acquaintance with Chelsea was fleeting. So, unfortunately, was George Eliot's. Her stay lasted less than three weeks and ended in death.

When George Eliot came to Chelsea in 1880 she was 61 and newly married to a much younger man, John Cross. She was at the height of her powers and had a string of successful novels behind her including *Adam Bede, The Mill on the Floss, Silas Marner* and *Middlemarch*. After Dickens's death she was regarded as Britain's leading writer admired, wrote the critic F.R. Leavis, for her 'luminous intelligence' and appreciated by Turgenev and Henry James.

Her earlier relationship with a married man, George Henry Lewes, with whom she lived, brought notoriety. They were shunned by polite society. Lewes, however, acted as her editor and literary agent and did much to promote her career. She had taken his first name as her own when deciding to use a pseudonym. Mary Ann or Marian Evans (she used various names) knew that male novelists were more highly acclaimed than female writers both critically and financially. 'I don't want the world to give me anything for my book except money,' she once wrote and drove a hard bargain with her publishers.

After George Henry Lewes died in 1878, she went through a period of depression, but a couple of years later married her financial adviser John Cross, who was 20 years her junior. The disparity in their ages proved too much. They were like mother and son and the marriage was unhappy. While on honeymoon in Venice, Cross tried to commit suicide by throwing himself off a hotel balcony into the Grand Canal, struggling to stay under water and drown as two gondoliers fought to rescue him. From that moment George Eliot never let him out of her sight.

On returning to London the couple moved to Number 4 Cheyne Walk. She was ill, but optimistic: 'I find myself in a new climate here,' she wrote, 'the London air and this particular house being so warm ... ' They had arrived in

Chelsea on 3 December, but a couple of weeks later she felt unwell during a concert. George Eliot was suffering from a kidney complaint. Three days before Christmas she died. Although their seven-month marriage failed, John Cross revered her memory and published a sympathetic biography.

Not everyone, though, was impressed by George Eliot. Oscar Wilde thought her style 'too cumbrous' and her novel, *Daniel Deronda*, the 'dullest of masterpieces'. Wilde himself came to Chelsea with his new wife, Constance, in 1885 and set up home at Number 16 (now 34) Tite Street. Already well known for his wit and poetry, his flamboyant personality had been satirized by Gilbert and Sullivan in their operetta, *Patience*. But his best work lay ahead. The ten years he spent in Chelsea would see his triumph on the London stage and the disastrous trials which led to the imprisonment that destroyed him.

Wilde was frequently in debt to tradesmen and the taxman. None the less he transformed his plain red-brick terrace home into a 'house beautiful'. Two friends, the artist James Whistler (who lived in the same street) and the architect and stage designer Edward Godwin, created an exotic interior. White paint predominated and the ceiling of the first-floor drawing-room was decorated with white peacock feathers. Down below on the ground floor, looking out on the street, was Wilde's library, Turkish or Moorish in style, with beaded curtains, wall hangings, lanterns and an inscription by Shelley exalting the 'Spirit of Beauty!' In this room Wilde did most of his writing, smoked and received friends – and enemies.

While Wilde was successful there was a constant stream of visitors – Ellen Terry, Arthur Balfour, Swinburne, Henry Irving, Lillie Langtry, Sarah Bernhardt. While in Chelsea he wrote *The Picture of Dorian Gray, Lady Windermere's Fan, Salome, A Woman of No Importance, An Ideal Husband* and his masterpiece, *The Importance of Being Earnest*.

But Wilde was living a double life. Although married with two children he divided his time between the theatre and louche young men, the most dangerous of whom, Lord Alfred Douglas, was the son of the ferocious Marquis of Queensberry. Drunkenness, suicide, lechery and madness ran in their family. The third marquis had murdered a kitchen boy and roasted him on a spit. The eighth marquis and his son, who brought about Wilde's ruin, inherited the family's destructiveness.

Wilde first met Douglas one afternoon in 1891 when a friend brought him to Tite Street, where he was shown into the library and offered tea. A few days later he was invited to Wilde's club.

*American writer Mark Twain spent
one of the unhappiest periods of his life
at 23 Tedworth Square between
1896–7.*

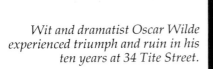

*Wit and dramatist Oscar Wilde
experienced triumph and ruin in his
ten years at 34 Tite Street.*

According to Douglas, Wilde made a pass at him, which he resisted, only to succumb a few months later.

Their relationship was soon the talk of society and the marquis outraged. Queensberry, who compiled the rules of boxing that bear his name, was like the villain in Victorian melodrama – abusive, quick to anger and violent. 'You impertinent young jackanapes,' he stormed at his son, 'if I catch you again with that man I will make a public scandal in a way you little dream of ... ' By the summer of 1894 he had had enough. On 30 June he turned up at Tite Street and demanded to see Wilde. He was shown into the library where Wilde said he stood with his back to the window shouting 'every foul word his foul mind could think of, and screaming the loathsome threats he afterwards with such cunning carried out'. He accused Wilde of 'disgusting conduct' and warned, 'If I catch you and my son together again in any public restaurant I will thrash you.' Wilde said he would shoot him on sight and summoned his servant to throw him out. 'This is the Marquis of Queensberry, the most infamous brute in London. You are never to allow him to enter my house again.'

From now on events whirled towards a terrible climax. The next year saw Wilde at the peak of his success. The premières of *An Ideal Husband*, which the Prince of Wales attended, and *The Importance of Being Earnest*, were triumphant. But Wilde's private life was catching up with him. When Queensberry left an insulting calling card at his club, Wilde prosecuted him for libel. During the court proceedings compromising letters were read out and a string of male prostitutes named, who were prepared to describe their relations with Wilde in salacious detail.

Wilde lost and the tables turned. Now he was open to prosecution for 'debauching' ... 'the liege subjects of our Lady the Queen'. Instead of fleeing the country, as friends advised, he went to the Cadogan Hotel in Sloane Street, where he sat drinking hock and seltzer. That evening there was a knock on his bedroom door. Two detectives arrested him and took him to Bow Street magistrates court.

After two more trials Wilde was finished. 'This is the worst case I have ever tried,' declared the judge, Mr Justice Wills, sentencing him to two years' hard labour. He was locked up in prison and the judge went back to his home (46 Tite Street), a few doors away from where Wilde had lived. Queensberry, meanwhile, forced the playwright into bankruptcy. The house beautiful was sold and ransacked, valuable manuscripts stolen and Constance and her two children driven out. Within five years of the trial Wilde was dead and so was the marquis.

Today the house, which is divided into flats, looks much the same outside as it did in Wilde's day, except for a plastic drain-pipe and a blue plaque.

Shortly after Wilde was dragged off to jail another distinguished author arrived in Chelsea in deep distress. Mark Twain had just heard his eldest daughter had died of meningitis in the United States. He was also in debt. All the money he had earned from *Huckleberry Finn* and *Tom Sawyer* had vanished after he had invested large sums in an unsuccessful typesetting firm. To earn money Twain set off on a round-the-world lecture tour. He arrived in Chelsea in the autumn of 1896 and stayed in a large Victorian corner house, 23 Tedworth Square, until the following July.

Grief-stricken Twain shut himself away from the world and to ease his sorrow concentrated on writing an account of his travels, *Following the Equator*. Later he admitted, 'I wrote my last travel book in hell.' That Christmas there were no celebrations. Sometimes he and his two remaining daughters would walk by the river and, on one occasion, he went to see Henry James who lived nearby in Kensington. In Chelsea he was unrecognized and walked the streets untroubled by admirers or well-wishers. On 18 February 1897 his notebook recorded: 'Walked for an hour in King's Road, as usual, between Markham Square and Chelsea Polytechnic, back and forth.' The people of Chelsea reminded him of 'Shakespeare people'.

His avoidance of publicity led to rumours in the United States that he was sick or dying. The London correspondent of the New York *Journal* was sent to find out. He had received a cabled instruction asking for 500 words if Mark Twain were ill and 1,000 if dead. It was then Mark Twain uttered his famous remark, 'Just say the report of my death has been greatly exaggerated.'

Close to Mark Twain lived another author, Bram Stoker, who published *Dracula* in 1897. Stoker created a cult figure known to millions world-wide – the blood-sucking vampire who dwelt in a coffin. 'There lay the Count ... the mouth was redder than ever, for on the lips were gouts of fresh blood, which trickled from the corners of the mouth and ran over the chin and neck ...'

All the repertoire of horrors beloved by B movie audiences were there – white vapour oozing out of a tomb, a corpse rising from the grave to drink the blood of the living, the creature 'with his cloak spreading out around him like great wings' that crawls face down a castle wall like a lizard, erotic women, howling wolves, violence and 'a vast ruined castle, from whose tall black windows came no ray of light, and whose broken battlements showed a jagged line against the moonlit sky'.

Stoker himself, despite an eye for the ladies, seems to have led a normal life. True his wife once found a corpse on her dining-room table when they lived at 27 Cheyne Walk, but there was an innocent explanation. Bram had rescued the man from the river, brought him home and called a doctor, but was too late to save him.

At the time *Dracula* was published Stoker lived at Number 18 St Leonard's Terrace, which bears a blue plaque to his memory.

Carlyle's hat.

Ecstasy in King's Road.

Nonchalance in King's Road.

Cooks in Chelsea Antiques Market.

Part of the fast disappearing Old Chelsea. The back garden of a restaurant in Sydney Street.

5   Books Without End

The greatest writer of humorous novels of his time, P.G. Wodehouse, started his career in Chelsea. During his life he published nearly one hundred books and countless articles, short stories, plays, musicals and lyrics. But during the two years he spent in Chelsea P.G. Wodehouse learnt the basic skills of his craft. 'My trouble, as with all beginning authors,' he said, 'was that I did not know how to write.' This was hardly surprising as he had just left Dulwich College and was still in his teens. In 1900 he had to earn a living in a City bank. Each morning and evening he would walk and sometimes run there from his small bed-sitter in Markham Square.

As a bank clerk Wodehouse was a failure. He found the job perplexing and cut a ridiculous figure in the financial world. His real interest lay in writing. Each night he returned to his 'horrible lodgings' off King's Road and wrote furiously, pouring out short stories (mostly for schoolboy magazines), articles and poems. The majority were rejected, but in two years he published eighty items. His largest fee was three guineas.

The publication of his first novel, *The Pothunters*, in 1902, encouraged him to leave banking and pursue writing as a career. In September he moved briefly to a large bed-sitter at the top of Number 23 Walpole Street where one night a visitor found him hard at work on a poem. Wodehouse was writing by the light of an oil lamp and was so cold he had wrapped a woollen sweater round his feet to keep warm.

The young author soon moved away from Chelsea and success came ten years later. The creator of Jeeves, Bertie Wooster, Psmith, innumerable intimidating aunts and eccentric aristocrats had a gradual climb to fame, but this came only after prodigious hard work and tenacity. Apart from an unfortunate incident in the Second World War, when the unworldly author was unwise enough to broadcast on German radio after he was captured by the Nazis, his career escaped controversy.

Changing the time, King's Road.

Radclyffe Hall, on the other hand, was enveloped by it. Her lesbian novel, *The Well of Loneliness*, caused outrage when it appeared in 1928. 'I would rather give a healthy boy or a healthy girl a phial of prussic acid than this novel,' wrote the editor of the *Sunday Express*, James Douglas. 'I have heard it whispered about by young men and young women who do not and cannot grasp its unutterable putrefaction ... The contagion cannot be escaped. It pervades our social life.'

A huge public row developed, copies of the book were seized in police raids and the publishers appeared in court. The magistrate was horrified at the novel's portrayal of 'two people living in filthy sin' and he condemned it for 'unnatural and disgusting obscenity'. Sales soared. Although *The Well of Loneliness* was banned in Britain, it was printed abroad. Copies were smuggled in from the Continent and it became a best-seller.

Before the scandal erupted Radclyffe Hall – or John as she was known – lived for 12 years (from 1907–19) with various women friends in Chelsea. She shared a flat near Harrods at 59 Cadogan Square with Mabel Batten, a woman twice her age. Later she fell in love with Admiral Troubridge's wife, Una, who abandoned her husband and moved in with John. They lived together for the rest of their lives and for a short time shared an apartment at 22 Cadogan Court, near Sloane Square.

Twenty years later the climate had changed. When *The Well of Loneliness* was republished in Britain in 1949 there was hardly a murmur. And, in 1974, BBC Radio broadcast the work nationwide in seventeen episodes in 'A Book at Bedtime'.

How different was the life of that master of the psychological novel and model of propriety, Henry James. He first came to Chelsea as a young man in 1869 and met the painter and poet Dante Gabriel Rossetti at his home in Cheyne Walk. James rediscovered Chelsea in 1911 when his secretary, Theodora Bosanquet, offered him two rooms in her flat at Number 10 Lawrence Street where he could work on his autobiography. The author liked his 'little Chelsea temple' and was charmed by the area. He appreciated its village-like atmosphere, bought items from the small shops and talked to local people. Life at Rye, in East Sussex, where he had a house, was depressing. He wanted to be near friends and the clubs of London. So, in 1913, he moved into a large flat overlooking the river, Number 21 Carlyle Mansions. 'This Chelsea perch, the haunt of the sage and the seagull,' he wrote, 'proves, even after a brief experiment, just the thing for me'. Battersea Park he found 'beguiling'.

On his 70th birthday Carlyle Mansions were crowded with

Carlyle Mansions, Cheyne Walk. Henry James died here, T.S. Eliot lived in flat 19 and Ian Fleming completed his first James Bond novel on a golden typewriter.

well-wishers. A golden bowl was presented to him and admirers arranged for Sargent to paint his portrait. When the First World War began the following year, James sided strongly with Britain, visited wounded soldiers in hospital and helped Belgian refugees who were housed nearby in Crosby Hall. He dined with the prime minister, Herbert Asquith, met Winston Churchill – a disaster; the young minister had no idea who he was and found him a bore – and at the height of the war, when Britain was most in danger, changed his nationality from American to British.

Then, on the morning of 2 December 1915, James collapsed with a stroke in his flat. 'It's the beast in the jungle, and it's sprung,' he gasped. For the next three months he slowly sank into oblivion. His mind wandered, the imaginary world of fiction mingling with the real world about him. Often he sat looking out on the river 'with the ever-creeping barges and low-lying clouds,' wrote his sister-in-law, Alice. 'He thinks he is voyaging and visiting foreign cities, and sometimes he asks for his glasses and imagines that he writes.'

While James lay on his deathbed, George V awarded him the Order of Merit, which brought comfort, but three months after he was struck down, James passed away. The funeral service took place in the Old Church, where a tablet marks his memory and his ashes were buried in the United States.

Henry James worked on a grand scale; Katherine Mansfield wrote short stories. On 2 March 1909 she married, but left her husband the same evening. She stayed at Number 131 Cheyne Walk from 1910–11, sleeping in a front room with a view of the river. Katherine used a human skull as a candle holder and installed a piano, though ill health made it difficult to practise. Two years after her first marriage she met John Middleton Murry and became his mistress. They were to marry in 1918, but the year before Katherine moved to a studio flat at 141A Old Church Street. This had a vast window filling the whole of one wall from floor to ceiling – 'my Thou-God-seest-Me window' she called it. Murry lived half-a-mile away at 47 Redcliffe Road.

'I am a recluse at present,' she wrote to the philosopher Bertrand Russell, 'and do nothing but write and read and read and write – seeing nobody and going nowhere.' That was an exaggeration. A friend brought her oysters, Aldous Huxley came round to chat and at a party one Sunday evening she met the new poet T.S. Eliot, Robert Graves and Roger Fry. Her friendship with Virginia Woolf began in the studio, though Virginia was soon jealous of her accomplishments and with typical Bloomsbury malice said she was 'hard' and 'shallow' and 'stinks like a civet cat'.

Katherine, whose work was compared to Chekhov's, revolutionized the short story. She was frequently ill, however, and tuberculosis killed her at 34. Besides her stories she left behind a mass of letters and a journal. Recognition was posthumous.

A.A. Milne was more fortunate. 'The poet laureate of the nursery' won fame in his lifetime. As a young man down from Cambridge he struggled as a freelance writer, taking two cheap, dirty rooms on the top floor of Number 8 Wellington Square. The house, owned by a policeman, was then an unfashionable address. Milne's fortunes soon changed after he joined the staff of the humorous magazine *Punch*. When he married in 1913 he and his wife moved to a flat at Number 15 Embankment Gardens. After the First World War they found a modern house at 11 Mallord Street (renumbered 13). By now Milne was a successful writer of comedies for the stage, including *Mr Pim Passes By*. At one time he had five plays running simultaneously. And it was while living at Mallord Street that he published four children's books that brought him instant fame – two volumes of verse – *When We Were Very Young* and *Now We Are Six*; and *Winnie-the-Pooh* and *The House at Pooh Corner*.

Their inspiration was his son Christopher Robin, who was born in the house in August 1920. His night and day nurseries were on the top floor. The teddy bear that became Pooh was a present from Harrods. Milne's American publisher, John Mcrea, remembered seeing the author and the artist Ernest H. Shepard, whose drawings contributed so much to the success of the books, at work in 1926 – 'Milne sitting on the sofa reading the story, Christopher Robin sitting on the floor playing with the characters, which are now famous in *Winnie-the-Pooh*, and, by his side, on the floor, sat E.H. Shepard making sketches for the illustrations which finally went into the book.'

Christopher Robin was unaware of their attentions, but later as an adult thought his father had exploited him. As the books became best-sellers the son became an international celebrity. When he walked to school in Tite Street or to Sloane Square passers-by would stare and whisper, 'That's Christopher Robin!'

Milne became increasingly jealous as his son stole the limelight. 'You can imagine my amazement and disgust,' he wrote, after visiting the United States, 'when I discovered that

A.A. Milne, creator of Christopher Robin and Winnie-the-Pooh, lived at 13 Mallord Street.

Katherine Mansfield's 'my Thou-God-seest-Me window' at 141a Old Church Street.

… I had been pushed into back place … It was this Christopher Robin, not I whom Americans were clamouring to see.'

By the fourth book Milne had had enough. He stopped writing about his son and toy animals and returned to adult work. But nothing afterwards was as successful. His children's books obliterated everything else. He became old, embittered and rich. His son was haunted by his younger self. As a teenager he was taunted at boarding school, the boys in the study next door playing over and over again a record of the poem *Vespers* he had made as a child. Eventually, he smashed it. He spent years as an adult trying to come to terms with his unearned fame.

Today a blue plaque marks the house in Mallord Street where A.A. Milne, Christopher Robin, Pooh, Piglet, Kanga and the other toys lived. But it tells nothing of the heartache that followed after the innocent delight of a child and his father was exposed to the world's gaze.

A blue plaque also marks the home of Arnold Bennett at Number 75 Cadogan Square. When he came to Chelsea in 1922 Bennett was a successful novelist with an unsuccessful marriage. He and his wife had separated, and his mistress, the actress Dorothy Cheston, had moved in. She was 30 years his junior and gave him a daughter. Bennett published between seventy and eighty books, among them *Anna of the Five Towns*, *The Old Wives' Tale* and the *Clayhanger* trilogy. While in Chelsea he wrote *Riceyman Steps* and *Imperial Palace*.

The former solicitor's clerk, who grew up in The Potteries, had come a long way. He had lived eight years in Paris, owned a yacht and mixed with the great.

Bernard Shaw came to lunch, though Bennett noted in his journal a few years before that he had fallen asleep while watching the first performance of *Back to Methuselah* at the Royal Court Theatre in Sloane Square – 'A most depressing night'. Noel Coward came to dine fresh from the success of his new play, *The Vortex*. The Maughams were invited. Bennett played tennis in the gardens with H.G. Wells (they were both in their 60s at the time) and the actress, Mrs Patrick Campbell, also in her 60s and voluble and noisy, burst in one evening and declared, 'If you want to keep me quiet give me a cigar.' So he did and out she went into the square smoking it.

When experiencing difficulty writing, Bennett strolled along King's Road to the Dairy Company's tea-shop, where he observed the antics of the customers and staff from behind a magazine. He maintained there was more lively comedy there than in a Parisian café. On New Year's night, 1924, he stormed out of the Chelsea Arts Club Fancy Dress Ball. Three or four thousand people were merrymaking – rowdy, uncouth and drunk. The noise was unbearable, the entertainment tacky and his chauffeur seemed 'to be a much superior person to most of the revellers'.

When the rent went up in 1930 Bennett moved out of Cadogan Square and found a flat in Baker Street where he died of typhoid a few months later.

While Arnold Bennett was living in affluence in Chelsea and enjoying the fruits of a successful career, the American writer, Thomas Wolfe, was struggling at the beginning of his. When he came to Chelsea in the autumn of 1926 he rented a first-floor flat at Number 32 Wellington Square, across the road from where A.A. Milne had lived a few years before. Wolfe was 25 and became known for vast autobiographical novels. These he wanted to 'swarm with life, be peopled by a city'. Before editing they ran to millions of words and while in New York he stored one of his manuscripts in a wooden crate. He began work on his first book, *Look Homeward, Angel*, in Chelsea. Drunken brawls alternated with spasms of writing and his rent was paid by his 45-year old mistress, Aline Bernstein, a successful stage designer who lived in New York with a husband and two teenage children. Wolfe first met her on the liner *Olympic* (sister ship of the *Titanic*) and they had made love while the ship lay at anchor off Staten Island waiting to enter New York harbour.

In 1926 they ran away together to Europe, made a lightning tour of England and Wolfe ended up in Chelsea when Aline returned to America. At 8.30 each morning the landlord would bring Wolfe his breakfast and newspaper, then the author would walk along the embankment and afterwards work until lunch-time. During the afternoon he went for 'enormous promenades through the East End of London', returned to Chelsea for a bath, went out for the evening and came back and wrote until midnight. By the end of a month he had completed the outline of his novel. On 4 October he left Chelsea and later sailed to the United States, arriving in time for Christmas, to be greeted by Aline jumping up and down on the jetty.

A few years later, in the 1930s, a young Welsh poet, Dylan Thomas, was hovering on the less salubrious borders of Chelsea. He shared a small room at 5 Redcliffe Street, near Brompton Cemetery. 'This is the quarter of the pseudo-artists', he wrote. He and his friends went to parties at the Royal

The American novelist Thomas Wolfe began work on his first novel, Look Homeward, Angel, *while living at 32 Wellington Square.*

Dylan Thomas's favourite pub, the Kings Head and Eight Bells. This riverside tavern has been popular with creative talent as diverse as Carlyle, David Frost, and Mick Jagger and Keith Richard of the Rolling Stones.

College of Art where they caused uproar. Dylan and his cronies drank large quantities of beer, dashed onto the dance floor, hurled themselves on the ground and rolled around screaming until they were dragged away. On their way home through Chelsea they climbed lamp-posts and shouted at passers-by. His drinking, though, was no joke. 'It ate up all our money and all our lives,' remarked his widow, Caitlin.

Dylan escaped fighting in the Second World War. From 1942–45 he wrote scripts for documentary films. At the beginning of this period he and his wife moved to Number 3 Wentworth Studios in Manresa Road. Their old flat had one room, with a glass roof that leaked when it rained and was dangerous in air raids – that and a bathroom and a kitchen hidden behind a curtain. Dylan and Caitlin's second child, Aeron, was born while they lived there.

In the evenings Dylan and his friends went off to the local pubs. Beer was in short supply in wartime, so they found out when and where the brewers made their deliveries and went to the pubs that were well stocked. The Australian was on their rounds, so was the Queen's Elm, where Dylan played billiards, and the Cross Keys. Dylan's favourite was the King's Head and Eight Bells, by the river at the corner of Cheyne Row and Cheyne Walk, a hundred yards from Carlyle's house. Here he played shove-halfpenny and darts and mixed with Bohemian friends. The pub was frequented by soldiers, sailors and airmen on leave. Dylan opposed the war and was unwise enough to tell them to lay down their arms and stop fighting. On one occasion a soldier knocked him down.

Drink killed Dylan before he was forty, just as he was winning popular acclaim. His studio was demolished to make way for modern houses, but the King's Head and Eight Bells is still there. The pub lies next door to Carlyle Mansions, the last home of Henry James and the home of another American-born writer, T.S. Eliot, who wrote what one critic called 'the most influential poem of our century in any language', *The Waste Land*. Eliot was a familiar figure in Chelsea for many years after the Second World War. When he came to the district in 1946 it was a time of deprivation. Everything was in short supply, rationing in force and sometimes water and electricity were cut off. The poet lived in monastic austerity. His bedroom resembled a monk's cell with a bare light bulb and crucifix over the bed and he ate his meals off a tray on his knees.

Eliot shared his flat with a disabled friend, John Hayward, who was confined to a wheelchair. John edited his poetry and

shared his enthusiasm for Sherlock Holmes. Eliot wheeled him to a King's Road restaurant to dine with friends, or took him over the Albert Bridge to Battersea Park. They also went for outings along the embankment to the Royal Hospital grounds, on one occasion watching a football match in the rain.

While he was living in Carlyle Mansions Eliot was awarded the Nobel Prize for Literature and the Order of Merit. He also learnt that his first wife had died. She had been confined to a mental hospital for years and caused him anguish. In the late 1940s and 50s Eliot looked like an old man burdened with care, but in 1957 he suddenly – and secretly – married his secretary, Valerie Fletcher. Despite the disparity in their ages – Eliot was 68, Valerie 30 – the marriage was successful. 'I am thinking of taking up dancing again,' he declared, and for the rest of his life knew happiness.

While at Carlyle Mansions Eliot occupied flat Number 19, on the third floor, directly beneath where Henry James and Ian Fleming lived. The creator of James Bond spent a year here in the early 1950s. As a child he had lived in Turner's house further up river, along with his brother, Peter, the travel writer. Their mother had struggled to bring them up after her husband was killed in the First World War. 'I am returning to childhood surroundings in Cheyne Walk!' Ian told his mother, in 1950, when he found rooms on the corner of Carlyle Mansions with 'terrific views up and down the river across London'.

It was a busy time for Fleming. He married, moved home and drafted the first James Bond novel while holidaying in Jamaica. He sensed he was writing something special and ordered a gold-plated typewriter. When he returned to London he locked himself in his bedroom in Carlyle Mansions and, without telling his new wife what he was doing, pounded away until *Casino Royale* was revised and publishable. His background of Eton, Sandhurst, Reuters, newspapers and Naval Intelligence during the Second World War was useful experience when writing about a glamorous spy. He produced a heady blend of fast action, snobbery, sex and sadism. Bond became a twentieth-century myth as potent as Sherlock Holmes, or Dracula.

Fleming's expertise was more tenuous than many imagined. A gunsmith prevented him publishing many errors about weapons in his first book and he consulted experts on cars, high finance and the Secret Service. 'His knowledge of food was erratic, of wine almost non-existent,' admitted his biographer, John Pearson. 'Only on matters of sex did he rely entirely on his own carefully guarded expertise.'

Chelsea Embankment with the Albert Bridge on the horizon –
the haunt of artists and writers from Rossetti and Henry James
to T.S. Eliot.

As for Bond, he too 'lived' in Chelsea, but Fleming left the exact location vague. The author tells us the spy had a comfortable ground-floor flat in a converted Regency house in a square off King's Road. Parked under the plane trees was his '1930 4½-litre Bentley coupé, supercharged, which he kept expertly tuned so he could do a hundred when he wanted to'.

The Bond books soon became a cult and by the time Fleming died in 1964 more than 40 million copies had sold. Opinions vary about their literary merit. The critic Anthony Burgess maintained Fleming was 'a distinguished writer of English prose'. But a rival in the field of spy fiction, John le Carré, dismissed Fleming as 'candyfloss' saying Bond was 'a consumer goods hero'.

Le Carré used Chelsea as a location in some of his serpentine stories. His mild-mannered secret agent, George Smiley, 'lived' in a Georgian cottage at Number 9 Bywater Street just off King's Road. 'I think I may have put him there,' he said, 'because a cul-de-sac is very difficult to keep under surveillance and Number 9 is well up at the blind end of Bywater Street.' In *Tinker, Tailor, Soldier, Spy* Smiley walks tentatively along the street, afraid to open his front door in case an enemy lurks within waiting to spring.

Two Chelsea pubs, the King's Head and Eight Bells, and the Balloon in Lots Road feature in le Carré's spy stories. In the first Smiley novel, *Call For The Dead*, Smiley corners a murderer, Dieter Frey, on a houseboat near Battersea Bridge. Le Carré said while writing the novel he 'moved from the country to Overstrand Mansions in Battersea, which may account for why I used Battersea Bridge for Frey's death'. It is pitch dark and raining with a thick yellow fog rolling up river when Dieter leaves the houseboat and makes for the bridge. A fight develops and Smiley forces him backwards over the parapet until he plunges into the black swirling waters and disappears. Distances are telescoped so descriptions are topographically inaccurate, but an author must be allowed artistic licence.

'Battersea was the nearest I got to living in Chelsea' admitted le Carré. The Poet Laureate, Sir John Betjeman, however, lived there at the beginning and end of his life. As a schoolboy he was taught by T.S. Eliot. Betjeman met 'the American master' as Eliot was called, while at Highgate School in 1916. Already he was writing poetry, but Eliot tactfully refrained from commenting on Betjeman's fledgling verse.

The following year when he was 11, John Betjeman moved to a small Georgian house at 53 Old Church Street in Chelsea,

*The 'home' of John le Carré's fictional spy George Smiley –
9 Bywater Street. The author chose this cul-de-sac off King's
Road as it made surveillance by enemies difficult.*

The Poet Laureate Sir John Betjeman in his cottage, 29 Radnor Walk.

The Albert Bridge, which Betjeman campaigned to save when it was threatened with demolition.

opposite the Old Rectory. 'Yes, the slummy end,' he sighed in his autobiographical poem *Summoned by Bells*. He and a friend used to explore London's churches, second-hand bookshops and the Underground.

Betjeman returned to Chelsea in 1977 when he was Poet Laureate and lived for the rest of his life in a cottage off King's Road at Number 29 Radnor Walk. By now he was famous, his books best-sellers and his enthusiasm for Victorian architecture no longer regarded as eccentric. He thought the shop fronts in King's Road 'vulgar', defended threatened buildings in the borough and complained about the demolition of the Chelsea Palace Theatre and its replacement by an unfortunate modern development. 'I'm always annoyed by improvements,' he once said. 'I feel genuinely wounded by mistakes people make.'

He championed suburbia, gas lamps, decorated architecture, buildings on a human scale and middle-class values, which he also satirized. *The Times* said he hastened 'the overthrow of that facile contempt for the recent past and for the achievements of the bourgeoisie, which after the war was so rapidly laying waste village, city and suburb with glass and chrome'.

Betjeman celebrated ordinariness. That was reflected in the cottage in which he lived, tiny in scale and crowded with memorabilia and – more disturbing – large insects in glass containers. But there was a darker side to Betjeman. While he delighted in the area he complained in his poem 'Chelsea 1977' of the smells, dog mess and sewage-pipes and made plain his fear of death – with Satan stoking hell-fire beneath the paving stones.

Antique shops tempt connoisseurs and the curious in King's Road.
Since the 1960s traditional shops have been driven out by fashionable
boutiques and restaurants.

A flavour of the old King's Road still remains.

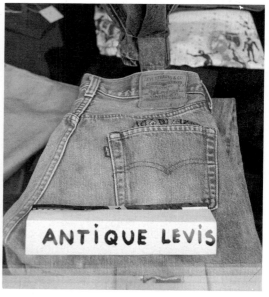

6   Chelsea Artists

Chelsea became the artists' quarter of London in the middle of the nineteenth century when Turner and Whistler arrived. Hundreds more followed and most of Britain's leading artists worked there during the next hundred years. When Turner arrived at Number 119 Cheyne Walk he was in his 70s. This master of landscape and water-colour found himself a cottage by the river with a boat builder on one side and a tavern on the other. Here he stayed with his landlady, Mrs Booth, an illiterate 'big loud coarse Scotchwoman', but a kindly soul who made him happy.

Turner lived in Chelsea incognito. Often he was mistaken for a seaman by local people. Tradesmen called him 'Admiral Booth' and youngsters 'Puggy'. Turner had a gallery built on the roof of his cottage where he could watch sunsets and fireworks at Vauxhall. Sometimes he was rowed up and down the river and over to Battersea where he observed the changing light. While living in Chelsea the artist painted his last four works for the Royal Academy. But his health was failing fast and he drank heavily and lived on rum and milk.

Turner died at ten in the morning just before Christmas 1851 in his small bedroom overlooking the Thames. Mrs Booth and his dentist, William Bartlett, were with him as he passed away. 'It was very dull and gloomy,' said Bartlett, 'but just before 9 a.m. the sun burst forth and shone directly on him with that brilliancy which he loved to gaze on and transfer the likeness to his paintings. He died without a groan.'

Over 300 of his paintings and 20,000 drawings and water-colour sketches remain, most of which are now housed in a special gallery down river at the Tate.

Turner painted shimmering light, fog, rain, hail and storms; Whistler preferred twilight. This American painter settled in London in 1859 and spent much of his life in Chelsea. From 1863–78 he lived near Battersea Bridge at Number 101 and later Number 96 Cheyne Walk. During his twelve years at Number

Battersea Reach, beloved by Whistler and Turner before him.

96 he painted some of his finest works, including the celebrated picture of his mother that hangs in the Louvre, a similar study of Carlyle, and other portraits.

In addition he painted Chelsea and the river – subtle impressionistic views of the little streets at twilight, snow scenes and delicate, misty studies of the Thames and Old Battersea Bridge that brought notoriety and disaster. Musical analogies in his titles provoked critics. 'Why should I not call my works "symphonies", "arrangements", "harmonies", and "nocturnes"?' he demanded. But it excited the wrath of John Ruskin who accused Whistler of 'flinging a pot of paint in the public's face'. The picture that enraged Ruskin was *Nocturne in Black and Gold: The Falling Rocket* depicting a firework display in Cremorne Gardens. Whistler sued Ruskin for libel and the painting was brought into the court upside down.

Whistler won the case, but was awarded only a farthing's damages and the costs bankrupted him. A new house he had built in Tite Street was sold to defray the expenses. From then on he lived at various addresses in Fulham and Chelsea and finally near the Old Church at 74 Cheyne Walk, where he died in poverty in 1903. But his reputation today is secure. 'No educated person,' wrote the critic James Laver, 'can walk along the bank of the Thames at nightfall without thinking of Whistler.'

Or indeed the Pre-Raphaelite poet and painter, Dante Gabriel Rossetti, who lived for twenty years at Number 16 Cheyne Walk. Rossetti was a sick and dying man, tormented by guilt and broken by drink and drugs. At night he would venture out of his house, sometimes accompanied by the young writer, Hall Caine, who remembered 'those nightly walks; the Embankment almost dark, with its gas-lamps far apart, and generally silent at our late hour, except for an occasional footfall on the pavement under the tall houses opposite; the black river flowing noiselessly behind the low wall and gurgling under the bridge; and then Rossetti in his slouch hat, with its broad brim pulled down low on his forehead as if to conceal his face, lurching along with a heavy, uncertain step, breathing audibly, looking at nothing, and hardly speaking at all'.

Rossetti, who had formed the Pre-Raphaelite Brotherhood with Holman Hunt and John Everett Millais, came to Chelsea in 1862. His wife, Elizabeth Siddal, who inspired some of his best work, had just died and he never recovered from her death.

When he first arrived in Chelsea he was accompanied by

The Rossetti memorial in front of his house, 16 Cheyne Walk.

The American painter John Singer Sargent worked 24 years in this studio at 31 Tite Street, where he died in 1925.

Dutch-style studio built for Augustus John at 28 Mallord Street. Later it was owned by the singer Gracie Fields.

During the 1940s Augustus John painted some of his most famous sitters in this studio at 33 Tite Street.

Algernon Swinburne and George Meredith, but they were driven away by Rossetti's eccentric behaviour. Wild parties and wild animals annoyed the neighbours. Wallabies bounced round the garden where armadillos burrowed under neighbouring walls and peacocks screeched.

Gradually Rossetti shut himself away from the world and became a recluse. Drugs killed him at the early age of 54. Today he is commemorated by a memorial fountain in the embankment gardens, directly in front of his house, and the Cadogan Estate has a special clause in its lease forbidding the keeping of peacocks.

The grandest painter to live in Chelsea was the American, John Singer Sargent, whose elegant studio at 31 Tite Street, attracted Oscar Wilde to the district. Henry James admired the painter and said Sargent had 'high talent, a charming nature, artistic and personal, and is civilised to his finger-tips'.

Sargent painted the kind of people James featured in his novels. His dazzling technique made him the most fashionable portrait painter of his day and society flocked to his studio which James described as 'opening upon a balcony that overhangs a charming Chelsea green garden'.

Sargent died at his studio in 1925. When he first arrived in London he had briefly used the studio next door at Number 33. This was later occupied for ten years by the 'King of the Bohemians,' Augustus John. He came to Tite Street in 1940 and went on painting throughout the air raids. One of his sitters, Constance Graham, recalled posing by the enormous studio window 'while the bombs buzzed overhead'. John was unperturbed and continued working.

He was commissioned to paint Britain's war leaders, including the victor of El Alamein, General Montgomery, who turned up at the studio before D-Day in 1944. Monty had heard of the artist's wild reputation and was suspicious. 'Who is this chap?' he demanded. 'He drinks, he's dirty, and I know there are women in the background!' The portrait confirmed his misgivings. He hated it.

Augustus John stayed at Tite Street until 1950. Before that he lived at various Chelsea addresses. In 1914 he built a Dutch-style house at Number 28 Mallord Street, behind which was a vast studio where he held riotous all-night parties. Early one morning in May 1921 a diffident young man turned up on his doorstep. He was Japanese and wanted a portrait of himself. Although it was eight o'clock John obliged and quickly dashed off a likeness. 'I was very much impressed by his

tranquil personality and natural dignity,' remarked the artist afterwards. 'He sat through the hour with complete ease.' The young man was the heir to the Japanese throne, Prince Hirohito, who was on a visit to London. Later as Emperor he was regarded by his subjects as a living god and was on the throne when Japan attacked Pearl Harbor – which brought the United States into the Second World War.

Augustus John left Mallord Street in the 1930s when a block of flats and telephone exchange were erected opposite, blocking out the light. He sold the house to the popular singer and comedienne, Gracie Fields. He is remembered now as a gifted artist and a character, but greatness eluded him. The Bohemian life-style overshadowed his art.

When it came to controversy, however, Augustus John was outdistanced by Jacob Epstein whose sculpture provoked violent attacks and even destruction. Before the First World War he worked in a studio near the Old Church at Number 72 Cheyne Walk. Epstein first sprang to notoriety when he carved eighteen statues for the British Medical Association building in the Strand. Critics claimed they were obscene, but Dr Cosmo Gordon Lang, later Archbishop of Canterbury, climbed the scaffolding for a closer inspection and declared there was nothing shocking about them. The controversy rumbled on for thirty years and eventually the critics won. When the building was taken over by the Southern Rhodesian government in the 1930s the figures were smashed. Their mutilated remains are still visible.

More controversy surrounded Epstein's monument for the tomb of Oscar Wilde. A twenty-ton block of stone was delivered to Cheyne Walk. Nine months later Epstein had carved a flying demon angel incorporating a portrait of Wilde. When this was transported to the Père-Lachaise cemetery in Paris where the playwright was buried there was uproar. A tarpaulin was thrown over the monument which was guarded by police who tried to stop the sculptor putting the finishing touches to his work. And when he carved the Hudson memorial in Hyde Park parliamentary pressure was applied to have it removed and the monument was daubed with paint and swastikas.

None the less the sculptor defeated the philistines. He published a peppery autobiography in which he rounded on his critics and was knighted in 1954. His Chelsea studio was destroyed by a parachute mine in 1941, when the Old Church was blown up, and one of Epstein's carvings now marks the site.

Green and Stone's art shop, King's Road, unchanged since 1934. Patronized by Augustus John, Francis Bacon and David Hockney. Formerly a suffragette shop.

7   The Music Makers

Startling as was the behaviour of many artists and writers who lived in Chelsea, it was equalled by the composer Percy Grainger whose bizarre private life contrasted starkly with his innocent music. Grainger admired Grieg who encouraged him to study folk-songs that lie at the heart of his popular works. Melodious and pithy compositions, such as *Country Gardens*, *Molly on the Shore*, *Mock Morris* (performed 500 times in 1913), *Shepherd's Hey* and *Handel in the Strand*, became part of the staple repertory of palm court orchestras, country fairs, school music and interludes on the wireless.

Grainger was an eccentric. He married before an audience of 20,000 at the Hollywood Bowl, had exotic tastes that would have delighted the Marquis de Sade, slept beneath a grand piano for fear of burglars and wanted his own skeleton put on public display when he died.

Grainger was 18 at the turn of the century when he and his mother arrived in London from Australia. A brilliant pianist, he travelled widely and lived at various addresses in Chelsea. Number 24 Coulson Street was their home in 1903, followed by 63 Oakley Street and 14 Cheyne Row. From 1908 until the outbreak of war in 1914, when he sailed to the United States, he lived near the Duke of York's headquarters at 31a King's Road. Grainger organized fortnightly musical evenings in his rooms where friends, including Ralph Vaughan Williams, sang and criticized each other's part songs.

Vaughan Williams, one of England's outstanding composers, had moved to Number 13 Cheyne Walk in 1905. There, for 24 years, he wrote many of his major and best-loved works – *On Wenlock Edge*, *The Wasps*, *A Sea Symphony*, the *Thomas Tallis* and *Christmas Carols Fantasias*, *The Lark Ascending*, *A Pastoral Symphony*, *The Mass in G Minor*, *English Folk* and *Sea Songs* and many others. 'His study was on the top floor,' said his second wife Ursula Vaughan Williams, 'and of course the trees were much smaller then so he had a wonderful view of the river,

A stone flautist decorates a Victorian home, Pont Street.

which he loved.' Indeed this partly inspired his *London Symphony* which incorporated the cry of a Chelsea lavender-seller. The study was piled high with books and manuscripts and had an out-of-tune upright piano against one wall.

When he came to Cheyne Walk, Vaughan Williams was reaching musical maturity. He was about to publish *The English Hymnal*, which he spent two years editing, 'a collection of the best hymns in the English language', he wrote, although the Archbishop of Canterbury was critical. The composer wondered whether his two years were wasted, but later realized this 'was a better musical education than any amount of sonatas and fugues'.

Tudor music and folk-songs were likewise an inspiration. Three months spent in Paris in 1908 studying orchestration with Maurice Ravel gave him 'a little French polish' and quickened his development. Ursula Vaughan Williams recalled a homely incident when the Frenchman came to Cheyne Walk. 'Ravel greatly enjoyed London and became, to Ralph's surprise, enchanted by such unlikely food and drink as steak and kidney pudding and stout.'

Another musical influence and personal friend, Gustav Holst, was a regular visitor, as were students from the Royal College of Music where Vaughan Williams taught composition.

Sadly, the composer's house was torn down in 1970 to make way for a modern development. There is now no Number 13 Cheyne Walk. Nor is there any memorial to Vaughan Williams in Chelsea. Only the black iron gate that guarded his front garden remains outside Number 14.

Vaughan Williams was one of the leaders of the twentieth-century revival of English music. So was Sir William Walton who spent his early years in Chelsea. Vaughan Williams had a brief encounter with the young composer at Oxford in 1920 when he examined him in music. As a student Walton was dilatory and was twice sent down, leaving the university without a degree. Disaster was averted by a friend, Sacheverell Sitwell, who recognized his intelligence and thought he needed help. Walton was invited to come to London and live with Sacheverell and his brother and sister, Osbert and Edith, and they more or less adopted him. He stayed at their home in Swan Walk, living off his friends for years, or as his wife put it 'sponging'. The Sitwells introduced him to the avant-garde art world and fashionable society, a remarkable piece of good fortune for a tongue-tied student, who played the piano badly and had grown up in Oldham.

All that survives of Ralph Vaughan Williams's home is his gate at 14 Cheyne Walk. The composer wrote his most popular music during his many years in Chelsea.

But Walton had talent. He took music seriously and, although he composed slowly, produced masterpieces. He was given an attic to work in and, according to Osbert Sitwell, used to eat cherries and throw stones out of the windows at passers-by.

When the Sitwells moved to Number 2 Carlyle Square Walton went with them and again took up residence in an attic. During November and December 1921 he wrote music to accompany Edith Sitwell's poems and together they produced the musical entertainment, *Façade*. The work was first performed a few weeks later in the first-floor drawing-room. Osbert found recitation embarrassing so a curtain was draped across the room. Behind it stood Walton conducting a quartet, fortified by sloe gin, while Miss Sitwell boomed her onomatopoeic verses through a giant papier-mâché megaphone. Snow lay thick on the ground, casting an eerie light into the room. The tiny audience of twenty or thirty people, who sat on gilded chairs, were nonplussed. Walton claimed they talked throughout the performance and regarded him and Edith as mad.

Façade was revised with more verse and music and later performed at the New Chenil Galleries, King's Road. Although parodied by Noel Coward and abused in the press it created less controversy at the time than the Sitwells later claimed. *Façade* was never hissed and booed by an audience, though many found it perplexing, or listened with indifference.

Walton lived at Number 2 Carlyle Square until the mid-1930s, by which time he had written his most popular works, *Portsmouth Point, Belshazzar's Feast* and *Symphony Number One*. But relations between him and the Sitwells became strained as he achieved success and independence. Eventually they turned on him and he moved out to pursue his musical career elsewhere, kept afloat by a legacy and increasing royalties from his music.

Unlike Walton and Vaughan Williams, Peter Warlock produced no large-scale works. Essentially a miniaturist, he is remembered mainly for his Elizabethan-style songs and minor orchestral pieces, such as the *Capriol Suite*.

Although gifted, Peter Warlock (or Philip Heseltine to give him his real name) was immature and emotionally unstable – a manic-depressive whose alternating moods provoked ridiculous excesses. On the one hand he was quiet, scholarly, witty and creative, on the other belligerent, extrovert and given to wild outbursts. He wrote stinging letters and articles, some of

Edith Sitwell's and William Walton's Façade *was first performed in the first-floor drawing-room of Sir Osbert Sitwell's house, 2 Carlyle Square.*

which provoked legal action, and made numerous enemies. D.H. Lawrence featured him as Halliday in his novel *Women in Love*. It was 'a malignant and scurrilous caricature,' wrote Warlock's biographer, Cecil Gray, 'extraordinarily venomous'. Warlock sued the publishers, the book was withdrawn and alterations made. He also appears as Coleman in Aldous Huxley's *Antic Hay*, where the more robust side of his character is displayed.

Warlock was born in the Savoy Hotel and spent his early years in Hans Road near Sloane Square. Later, as an adult, he moved to Bramerton Street and a flat at Number 30 Tite Street, a couple of doors away from Oscar Wilde's former home. He was hopeless with money and worked in fits and starts. Cecil Gray said that like the eighteenth-century Italian composer, Antonio Sacchini, 'He was unable to write music unless surrounded by cats and mistresses' and there was an abundant supply of both.

Warlock admired and frequently corresponded with Delius, but a letter in 1913 contained a chilling prophecy. 'I cannot but feel,' wrote Warlock, 'that I am an absolutely useless specimen in every branch of life – only fit, as I am, for a lethal chamber ... '

He behaved outrageously at parties, drank heavily and landed in court. The composer also dabbled in the occult and black magic, experimented with drugs and broke into acrobatic dances in public places – on restaurant tables, in pubs, Piccadilly Circus and Charing Cross Station.

By his mid-thirties it was obvious Warlock's muse had flown. Musically he was repeating himself and there was little public recognition. He was a failure. Shortly before Christmas 1930 a strong smell of gas was noticed coming from his flat. The police were summoned and Warlock was found unconscious on the sofa. He was dead. A kitten was discovered prowling around outside in the yard. Warlock had let it out of his flat before turning on the gas taps. Although an open verdict was reached at the inquest friends were convinced he had committed suicide. He was 36. His last home, which contained the lethal chamber, is marked by a blue plaque.

The Pheasantry, King's Road, named after birds that were bred here in the nineteenth century. The building was later used by the Russian Dancing Academy. Diaghilev was a guest and Anton Dolin, Alicia Markova and Margot Fonteyn pupils. Now a restaurant, it was once a club frequented by artists such as Augustus John and Pietro Anigoni and actors including Gregory Peck and Peter Ustinov.

8 Stars of Stage and Screen

Chelsea has always been popular with actors, actresses and stage and film directors. The actor-manager, Sir Herbert Beerbohm Tree, lived in Sloane Street in the 1890s. He was a great character actor, but had difficulty in remembering lines. One colleague recalled prompters were stationed 'under tables, behind rocks, jutting walls or ancient oaks as he moved in well-disguised anguish from cache to cache'.

A short time later the irascible W.S. Gilbert, who wrote librettos for Sir Arthur Sullivan's light operas, moved to Number 52 Pont Street, close to where Mrs Patrick Campbell had her last London home (Number 64).

Close by at Number 21 lived Lillie Langtry, the royal mistress turned actress. She was so beautiful people stood on chairs to see her when she entered a room. Although married, she was spotted by the Prince of Wales (later Edward VII) and became his paramour in 1877, the affair lasting until 1881 when she went on the stage. Mrs Langtry came to Pont Street in 1892 and had a machine installed that printed out the latest racing results. In her entrance hall stood an enormous stuffed grizzly bear, rearing up on its hind legs, teeth bared and as tall as a man, holding a tray for visiting cards in its paws. Mrs Langtry stayed in Pont Street until 1897 and her home is now incorporated into the Cadogan Hotel. Later she moved to Number 2 Cadogan Place. Her husband was reduced to bankruptcy by her extravagance.

The great Shakespearian actress Ellen Terry lived at 215 King's Road from 1904–20 in the house once owned by Thomas Arne and later occupied by Peter Ustinov in the 1950s. The house next door, Number 213, was for thirty years the home of Sir Carol Reed. He moved there in 1948 and directed classic films such as *Odd Man Out*, *The Fallen Idol* and *Our Man in Havana*. He clashed on the set with Orson Welles while directing *The Third Man*. Reed also tried to direct Marlon Brando in *Mutiny on the Bounty*, but the Hollywood star proved so difficult to handle

The Royal Court Theatre, Sloane Square, home of the English Stage Company. Here Bernard Shaw's plays were first performed and John Osborne's Look Back in Anger.

that he abandoned the film and returned his fee. He directed a few more films including *The Agony and the Ecstasy*, with Charlton Heston, and the musical *Oliver!*, but his career never recovered and he died sad and disillusioned in 1976. His funeral was held in Chelsea Old Church. From the balcony came the sound of a zither playing the *Harry Lime Theme* that had featured in *The Third Man*.

Further down King's Road the comedienne, Joyce Grenfell, set up home 'for ten happy but deafening years' in a flat over a shop. It was directly opposite a bus stop and she had to close the window before she could speak on the telephone. Joyce used to plan her reviews, broadcasts and theatrical appearances in her kitchen dining-room, but in 1956 was driven from her home by traffic noise. For the rest of her life, until she died in 1979, she lived in a flat at 34 Elm Park Gardens.

Britain's greatest actor, Laurence Olivier, lived in or near Chelsea for half a century. After marrying his first wife Jill Esmond, in 1930, they moved to Whistler's last riverside home, 74 Cheyne Walk, close to Crosby Hall. The house had a large studio at the back, with a minstrel's gallery, where the Oliviers entertained.

But in the spring of 1936 Olivier met the actress Vivien Leigh, who was newly married. They promptly fell in love and a few months later made their first film together, *Fire Over England*. They were so infatuated with one another that when Olivier's wife gave birth to their son he invited Vivien to the christening party in their Cheyne Walk studio. They arrived arm in arm, Vivien sporting a scarlet sweater.

Soon they were living together. Olivier abandoned his wife and, in 1937, took a lease on Durham Cottage at Number 4 Christchurch Street. The cottage, locked away behind white-washed walls with a blue and white wooden door leading from the street to the front garden, made a comfortable love nest. Vivien converted it into a fashionable home, filled with flowers and pictures by Degas, John Piper and Sickert. Cupids decorated the headboards of their oversized beds. To the public they were perfect lovers.

After moving in they organized a Guy Fawkes' party. Ralph Richardson, who was appearing on stage at the Old Vic with Olivier in *Othello*, was invited and brought his own supply of rockets. These he set up in the drawing-room, aiming them through the curved windows into the garden. Unfortunately he miscalculated. Once lit the rockets took off, swerved out of control and ran up the curtains, filling the room with sparks and

Durham Cottage, 4 Christchurch Street, home of Laurence Olivier and Vivien Leigh from 1937–56. While here the couple won international fame and Olivier was knighted.

Judy Garland died in this cottage at 4 Cadogan Lane soon after she married for the fifth time in 1969.

The Artistic Director of the Royal Court Theatre, Max Stafford-Clark in rehearsal.

smoke. Everyone was horrified and Ralph left in disgrace.

Vivien and Olivier married in 1940. The same year she was awarded an Oscar for her role as Scarlett O'Hara in the Hollywood film *Gone With the Wind*. This she kept on the mantelpiece in the living-room at Durham Cottage, a source of jealousy for Olivier until he won two Oscars for his films *Henry V* and *Hamlet*. All three awards were then placed on a bookcase in their bedroom.

They set off for a tour of Australia in 1948, but before departing seventy guests came to a farewell party that went on until five in the morning. Danny Kaye scraped white paint off their wall as he drove away in his car.

But all was not well with the Olivier's marriage. Soon after their return in 1949 Vivien told her husband she no longer loved him. She broke the news while they were sitting in the small winter-garden porch at Durham Cottage. The marriage staggered on for another decade, but in 1956 they moved from the cottage to Eaton Square and divorced in 1960.

Later Olivier lived at Number 7 St Leonard's Terrace and at the end of his life had a home in Mulberry Walk.

Judy Garland's life ended in nightmare. The Hollywood star made her name in 1939 in *The Wizard of Oz*, in which she sang the song that became her signature tune, *Over the Rainbow*. When she came to Chelsea thirty years later she was exhausted, sick, drank heavily and took up to seventy pills a day – pep pills, tranquillizers and sleeping tablets – a lethal cocktail that destroyed her talent, made public performances impossible and killed her. 'What do I do when I'm down?' she once asked. 'I put on my lipstick, see my stockings are straight and go out there and sing *Over the Rainbow*.'

On 15 March 1969 she went to Chelsea Registry Office at the Old Town Hall and married her fifth husband, Mickey Deans. It was a sad affair. Judy had a row with reporters outside and later at the reception only fifty guests turned up after hundreds had been invited.

She and her husband went to live in a mews cottage near Knightsbridge, Number 4 Cadogan Lane. The marriage was turbulent. They had furious rows and sometimes Judy collapsed. After a Scandinavian concert tour the unhappy couple returned to their Chelsea home. On Saturday 21 June they went to bed and Deans was woken next morning by the phone ringing. There was no Judy beside him. Deans got up, went to the bathroom, found the door locked and hammered on it. Fearing the worst, he climbed out of a window on to part of the roof where he could see into the bathroom. Judy was sitting down and appeared to be asleep. Deans prised open the window and crawled inside. Judy was dead.

The coroner said she had died from an accidental overdose of sleeping tablets. She was 47.

The British film star, Kenneth More, also came to a sad end in Chelsea. In the 1950s he was Britain's most popular film star with a string of successes to his name – *Geneviève*, *Reach for the Sky* (where he played the crippled wartime fighter pilot Douglas Bader), *The Admirable Crichton* and *A Night to Remember*, about the sinking of the *Titanic*.

He and his new wife, the actress Angela Douglas, moved to Chelsea in 1978 and lived briefly in a flat and then a house off King's Road. By coincidence their house was a short distance from Sir Thomas More's estate, which was appropriate as Kenneth was a direct descendant of the Tudor statesman. Four hundred years later the family likeness was still visible in the actor. Although proud of his ancestor Kenneth never exploited the link. But he had a Holbein print of Sir Thomas on his wall at home and paid a private visit to the cell where Sir Thomas was imprisoned in the Tower of London.

Shortly after Kenneth More moved to Chelsea he was struck down by Parkinson's disease. 'I have to admit I feel like Hell,' he told a newspaper just before he died in 1987. 'I have a lot of time with my thoughts these days and sometimes they hurt so much I can hardly bear it.'

Chelsea has happier associations, however, for many actors. Normally it is a good place to work. According to the theatre, opera and film director Sir Peter Hall, 'The Church Hall at Chelsea Old Church, Petyt House, is one of the pleasantest places to rehearse in London.' He used it in 1989 while rehearsing *The Merchant of Venice*, with Dustin Hoffman and Geraldine James, and in 1980 worked there with Vanessa Redgrave on *Orpheus Descending*. He returned in 1990 to rehearse Ibsen's *The Wild Duck*. Harold Pinter and Simon Gray have also worked in Petyt House. 'People always think that rehearsals are conducted in a theatre,' said Sir Peter. 'They are not. They usually are conducted in a cold, dark, cramped space which is as cheap as possible. Petyt House gets us out of that problem. It is quiet, roomy, light and in an attractive area.'

It is also out of the way, and the comings and goings of famous actors pass unnoticed, unlike their appearances on stage at the Royal Court Theatre at the other end of Chelsea in Sloane Square. The theatre was founded in 1888 and between

1904–7 Harley Granville-Barker and his team put on 32 plays by 17 authors. The Royal Court staged many of the first performances of Bernard Shaw's plays, including *Candida, John Bull's Other Island, Major Barbara* and *Heartbreak House*. And the theatre put on works by Ibsen, Yeats, Galsworthy and Maugham.

It was bombed in 1940 but rebuilt after the war. In 1956 George Devine created the English Stage Company who performed the first production of John Osborne's *Look Back in Anger*, which transformed British drama. The 'Angry Young Men' had arrived. Plays by Arnold Wesker, Harold Pinter and other innovators followed and the Royal Court also staged the first production of *The Rocky Horror Show* which has since become a cult.

The theatre's Artistic Director since 1979, Max Stafford-Clark, said during its first hundred years seasons of radical innovation alternated with periods when the Royal Court's influence was marginal. His twenty years of working in the theatre had coincided with a 'golden period of writing for the English stage. In this time the theatre, led by the English Stage Company, has made itself part of the debate English society has with itself about how it will live.'

The actress Lillie Langtry,
Edward VII's mistress, lived at
21 Pont Street.

9   Café and High Society

When *Look Back in Anger* was premièred in Chelsea John Osborne was unknown. His script was rejected by more than two dozen managements before it was staged at the Royal Court. After a slow beginning the play caught on and Osborne became a national figure. The following year he married the actress, Mary Ure, who appeared in one of the leading roles in the play. The ceremony took place at Chelsea Registry Office, the scene of many show business and fashionable weddings. 'We both have the strongest possible objections to marrying in church,' declared the couple after the ceremony. 'We loathe all clergymen.'

A cleryman's son, the television personality David Frost, married there in 1983. So did what one biographer called 'the century's most infamous woman', Wallis Simpson who induced King Edward VIII to abdicate, and became the Duchess of Windsor. In 1928 she married the American-born Englishman Ernest Simpson. Both were newly divorced and this was their second marriage. The wedding took place at eleven o'clock in the morning on 21 July. It was sunny and warm and the bride wore yellow, but the registry office was a dark Victorian building and Mrs Simpson complained about its 'grimy' corridors and said, 'The setting was more appropriate for a trial … ' She and Ernest were married in an untidy office by a bored official. It was 'a cold little job', Ernest later remarked.

Ernest introduced his wife to English society and this led to her fatal entanglement with the Prince of Wales. Royal connections made her a target for society hostesses. Soon she was on intimate terms with that 'sensitive barometer of fame', Lady Sibyl Colefax. She was the wife of a lawyer and made a fortune from interior decorating, living from 1922–37 in an elegant Georgian mansion, Argyll House, at Number 211 King's Road. Laurence Olivier, who asked her to decorate

Spring in Christchurch Street.

Durham Cottage, described Lady Colefax as the 'Queen of hostesses'. At luncheon and dinner parties she gathered glittering people of the day. She rose at five in the morning and wrote invitations by hand for three hours. The art critic and historian, Kenneth Clark, said if someone dropped out at the last moment 'she would suffer a physical change, the upper part of her face would turn black. She literally gave one a black look and it was very alarming.'

Lady Colefax had a penchant for royalty, major political figures and theatrical and literary celebrities. The diplomat, Robert Bruce Lockhart, claimed she knew Mrs Simpson better than anyone. And it was at Argyll House in the mid-1930s that Mrs Simpson first met Winston Churchill, then a backbench MP at the nadir of his fortunes. He told her it was the first time he and his wife had been invited out that year since his break with the Tory leadership. On another occasion Churchill was seen arguing fiercely with the chairman of the J.P. Morgan bank about British debts owed to the United States while the chancellor of the Exchequer, and later prime minister, Neville Chamberlain, sat glum and silent.

Among those who came to Argyll House was Bernard Shaw, Rudyard Kipling, H.G. Wells, Rebecca West, Arnold Bennett, Noel Coward, the Duff Coopers, Somerset Maugham, Virginia Woolf, the Sitwells (who abused Sibyl behind her back and called her 'old Coalbox'), Max Beerbohm, the Mosleys (then still respectable) and a young naval officer, Lord Louis Mountbatten. Charlie Chaplin entertained her guests with descriptions of elderly New York bankers who imitated his antics on the screen to amuse their children. Cecil B. de Mille and the American journalist, Walter Lippmann, were also invited. John Gielgud remembered Gertrude Lawrence bursting into the dining-room and sweeping down in a low curtsy before someone she thought was the Duke of Kent, only to find out that he was a columnist from the *Daily Express*.

On 13 December 1935, a few weeks before George V died, Ernest and Wallis Simpson arrived, along with the Prince of Wales. By now the Prince and Mrs Simpson were close friends, some said lovers, but the public were unaware of anxious gossip circulating in the government and high society as British newspapers remained silent. Earlier in the summer Bruce Lockhart had attended a dinner at Lady Colefax's. The Prince talked eagerly about friendship with Hitler's Germany and Lockhart noted in his diary that he had 'never heard him talk so definitely about the subject before'.

In the 1930s Edward VIII, Mrs Simpson and Winston Churchill were guests at sumptuous parties in Argyll House, 211 King's Road. They were organized by the society hostess Lady Sybil Colefax.

When Sibyl's husband died she sold Argyll House. Before leaving, however, she organized her grandest party in the summer of 1936. By now the Prince of Wales had become King and was hoping Mrs Simpson would become Queen. Edward VIII and Wallis arrived at Argyll House that evening with remarkable little ceremony – not even an aide-de-camp in attendance, but the occasion was marred by royal discourtesy. When the pianist, Artur Rubinstein, played Chopin the King became restive and decided to leave early. According to Kenneth Clark and the author and diplomat, Harold Nicolson, there was consternation. Only the arrival of Winston Churchill delayed the royal departure. Noel Coward was persuaded to sing *Mad Dogs And Englishmen* and *Don't Put Your Daughter On The Stage, Mrs Worthington*. The King heard him, returned to the party and stayed until late.

The King and Mrs Simpson were six months away from disaster. Before the end of the year he was forced to abdicate as he insisted on marrying her. The pair spent the rest of their lives in exile as the Duke and Duchess of Windsor – banished from the high society that once craved their company.

Argyll House is still there, hidden from traffic behind a high brick wall. Next door at Number 213 in a smaller Georgian house, lived another society hostess – and rival – Syrie Maugham. She was the estranged wife of the novelist, Somerset Maugham, and was unlucky in love. She turned to interior decorating to earn a living. 'Syrie Maugham,' declared *Vogue*, 'was *the* society decorator.' It was she who introduced snow-white interiors and her Chelsea home contained a dazzling white drawing-room where she held an 'all-white party'. She also introduced the corner sofa, which divided into two separate pieces of furniture – 'a wise precaution in these days when people move on', observed *Vogue*.

Syrie's manner was regal and imperious. She rode everywhere in a chauffeur-driven Rolls-Royce and expected to be obeyed. She had an explosive temper and hurled shoes at people who annoyed her. When she found some wall coverings were too short she lowered the height of a ceiling without telling the client.

Syrie attracted café rather than high society, maintained the photographer Sir Cecil Beaton. As many as 200 people crowded into her home for a party. 'Anyone might be there: Royalty, anyone at all.' And that included the Prince of Wales, who arrived one evening carrying his own bottle of champagne. The food was superb, champagne and wine flowed and the flowers were glorious, but by 1936 it was all over and Syrie moved to nearby Belgravia.

After the Second World War another Prince of Wales came to Chelsea, though he escaped the scandals surrounding his predecessors. Prince Charles (then the Duke of Cornwall) was eight at the time and the first British heir to the throne to go to school. 'Mummy, what are schoolboys?' he asked the Queen shortly before he went to his first school in Chelsea. He found out at 9.15 on the morning of 28 January 1957 when he arrived in a Ford car at Hill House School in Hans Place, a few minutes drive from Buckingham Palace. The Prince was greeted on the pavement by the headmaster, Colonel Henry Townend. He was called 'Charles' by the boys and 'Prince Charles' by the teachers. 'He had to take his chance with the other boys,' declared the headmaster, 'having his milk in the middle of the morning, his lunch and taking the same subjects as the other boys in his class.'

Sometimes the young Prince was spotted walking with his classmates through the Chelsea streets, or playing football at the Duke of York's headquarters, in King's Road, where a sports day was held in the summer. The Queen and Duke of Edinburgh watched with other parents as Prince Charles played football, handball-rugger and cricket, applauded by his sister, Princess Anne. 'In the gun drill,' the *Manchester Guardian* reported, 'a team of six, including Prince Charles, had to manoeuvre a light-weight model of an eighteen pounder field gun across a 20 ft chasm represented by steel scaffold poles on the grass. The Prince was the first of his team to swing himself across the chasm on a steel bar, 8 ft from the ground – an effort which was again applauded by Princess Anne.'

In the autumn Charles moved to Cheam School, in Hampshire, but twenty years later his future bride, Lady Diana Spencer, came to live in Chelsea. She returned from a finishing school in Switzerland in March 1978 and spent the first few weeks in her mother's house, Number 69 Cadogan Place, a few doors from where the prime minister, Harold Macmillan, had lived in his youth. In the summer she came back and for the next year stayed at the same address with friends. Lady Diana was 17. She learnt to drive and for three months could be spotted at Sloane Square Underground station each morning waiting for a train to take her to Wimbledon where she was studying cookery.

In January 1979 she met the Prince of Wales at Sandringham. Later he phoned her at Cadogan Place inviting her out to the

*Colonel Henry Townend presides over morning assembly at Hill House
School where the Prince of Wales was once a pupil.*

ballet and opera. Otherwise she liked dinner parties at home and went out to Chelsea restaurants with friends. Eventually Lady Diana moved to a flat just across the border in Kensington and lived there until her marriage to the Prince in 1981.

Chelsea saw another fateful royal encounter in 1958. On 20 February the Queen's sister, Princess Margaret first met a young photographer, Tony Armstrong-Jones, at the Chelsea home of one of her ladies-in-waiting, Lady Elizabeth Cavendish. Two years later they married in Westminster Abbey and Mr Armstrong-Jones was created the Earl of Snowdon. The marriage was unhappy and was dissolved in 1978.

Their son, Viscount Linley, has proved enterprising. In 1988 he and the photographer, Lord Lichfield, created Deals restaurant at Chelsea Harbour. As the harbour was still under construction and unknown to most Londoners 500 taxi drivers were invited to the opening

In Chelsea even dogs can expect to travel in style.

10   Heroes and Villains

Chelsea has had more than its fair share of heroes, villains and politicians, some of whom have had tragic or violent ends. The nineteenth-century engineer, Sir Marc Brunel, and his son Isambard Kingdom, who built on an heroic scale, lived in Lindsey House at Number 98 Cheyne Walk from 1808–25. Isambard designed the Great Western Railway and what was for decades the world's largest ship, *The Great Eastern*, a brilliant concept dogged by mishaps that hastened his death.

General Gordon was killed at Khartoum in 1855 – according to legend at the top of a staircase in his palace brandishing a revolver and sword. For a short time he rented rooms at Number 114 Beaufort Street during his stay in Chelsea a few years before.

The Antarctic explorer, Robert Falcon Scott, made his home at 56 Oakley Street. He too ended tragically. After making his name in HMS *Discovery*, when he explored the Antarctic from 1900–4, Scott embarked on a second expedition. This time he wanted to reach the South Pole, but when he arrived on 17 January 1912 he found a Norwegian expedition under Amundsen had beaten him by a month. Scott and the rest of his party perished in the snow.

Admiral of the Fleet, Earl Jellicoe, also came to Chelsea. He was Commander-in-Chief of the Grand Fleet in 1916 when the British Navy encountered the German High Seas Fleet. Winston Churchill said, 'Jellicoe was the only man on either side who could lose the war in an afternoon.' The admiral was, therefore, cautious. Two-hundred-and-fifty ships and twenty-five admirals engaged in the Battle of Jutland, but the result was inconclusive. The British lost more ships than the Germans who claimed victory, but the German ships broke off the action and sped back to base. They never again threatened Britain's

Margaret Thatcher's former home in Flood Street.

supremacy of the seas. Some people, however, never forgave Jellicoe for failing to deliver a knock-out blow.

The admiral lived at Number 25 Draycott Place, near Sloane Square. By coincidence he was close to Tryon Street. This was named after Admiral Sir George Tryon who drowned in the Mediterranean in 1893, after ordering his fleet to perform dangerous high-speed manoeuvres. His iron-clad, HMS *Victoria*, sank with the loss of over 300 lives. On board was Jellicoe, who was ill in his cabin when the accident happened. He escaped and said the disaster cured his illness. 'The ducking did me good,' he wrote to his mother.

Arguably the most important political figure to live in Chelsea was the founder of Communism, Karl Marx. He 'had more influence in less time than anyone else in history', wrote Bryan Magee. 'Within a mere seventy years of his death a third of the human race was living under governments that called themselves by his name.'

Marx was forced out of one country after another because of his revolutionary activities and eventually came to London in 1849. He spent more than half his life in exile in Britain where he wrote his greatest work *Das Kapital*. One of his first homes was a two-room flat at Number 4 Anderson Street, a few yards from King's Road. His fourth child was born there, but the family's stay lasted only six months as they ran out of money. Marx was evicted for failing to pay the rent – £6 a month.

Paradoxically, the man who spent much of his life analysing capitalism was unable to handle his own finances. His mother said she wished Karl would make some capital instead of writing about it. Eventually there was a day of reckoning in Chelsea. Local tradesmen complained of unpaid bills. His wife Jenny wrote in a letter, ' ... two bailiffs came and sequestrated all my possessions – linen, beds, clothes, everything, even my poor child's cradle and best toys of my daughters, who stood weeping bitterly'.

The next day they were forced to leave. Their beds were sold to pay the rent and a huge crowd gathered to watch. 'In less than five minutes,' wrote Jenny, 'there were two or three hundred persons loitering around our door – the whole Chelsea mob.'

Marx lived at various London addresses and died in 1883 virtually unknown, but gradually his influence spread until it became world-wide in the next century.

With David Lloyd George it was different. Once internationally renowned, this brilliant politician described as 'the cleverest prime minister this century', is now almost forgotten. Lloyd George's achievements were formidable. While at the Board of Trade (1905–8) he carried out a host of welfare reforms. Later as chancellor of the Exchequer he introduced old age pensions.

Lloyd George was adept at settling or averting strikes by miners, dockers and railwaymen. At the height of the First World War, when the British government was faltering, he seized power as prime minister and brought victory. He was one of the 'Big Three' at the Paris peace negotiations and to a large extent shaped the controversial Treaty of Versailles (1919) – the most important of the treaties that ended the First World War. He partitioned Ireland in 1921.

When he rented a house at Number 5 Cheyne Place in January 1908 he was still president of the Board of Trade. But in April the prime minister, Herbert Asquith, appointed him second man in the cabinet – chancellor of the Exchequer. Lloyd George immediately informed the editor of the *Daily Chronicle* before an official announcement from Downing Street. The prime minister was furious, but typically Lloyd George sent him a letter denying all.

Lloyd George had few friends. He was unscrupulous and opportunistic. Eventually his duplicity and controversial policies brought him down. After 1922 he never again held high office. For a number of years he lived on the embankment at Number 10 Cheyne Walk (the next occupant was an archbishop). Like Walpole he was one of the few prime ministers to leave office substantially richer than he went in. Few trusted him and he declined into a shabby old age.

The reverse happened to the Conservative prime minister Harold Macmillan, whose reputation was enhanced as he grew older. He was born in 1894 at Number 52 Cadogan Place. His parents lived there for fifty years and in his memoirs Macmillan drew a lively picture of life in Chelsea at the turn of the century. The family had half a dozen servants. The house was tall and thin; everything, including food and coal, had to be carried up from the kitchen in the basement to the nursery at the top. Harold Macmillan recalled the lamp-lighters at work in the evenings and the noise of a hammer on an anvil at the back in Cadogan Mews where a blacksmith made shoes for horses. London was like a country town with horse-drawn vehicles clattering along cobbled streets. 'Dung, straw, and sparrows were everywhere.'

Macmillan spent three years between the ages of six and nine at Mr Gladstone's day-school, near Sloane Square, where he received a good grounding in Latin and Greek. On Sundays he worshipped in Holy Trinity Church, Sloane Street.

As a schoolboy the young Macmillan was anything but the calm, unflappable figure he appeared to be when he held high government office. Throughout his life he suffered from depression and nervous breakdowns. He was convinced some 'mysterious power' was out to get him. 'One felt that something unpleasant was more likely to happen than anything pleasant.'

It did. Ill health forced him to leave Eton after only three years and his time at Oxford was cut short by the First World War. In 1916 he was severely wounded in the Battle of the Somme. He arrived at Victoria Station exhausted and dangerously ill with shrapnel in his right knee and his pelvis riddled with machine-gun bullets. None the less he had the presence of mind of persuade the ambulance driver to take him home to Cadogan Place, rather than to a military hospital where he might have died. His mother came to the door, was appalled and immediately drove him to a nearby private hospital. 'She literally saved my life,' he wrote. Recovery was slow. He underwent numerous operations and was in and out of hospital for years. The shuffling walk and limp handshake, which were the butt of satirists when he was prime minister, were the result of war wounds from which he never recovered.

Harold Macmillan is remembered with affection. The most hated political figure to live in Chelsea was the radio traitor William Joyce, Lord Haw-Haw. He went to Germany when the Second World War broke out and broadcast Nazi propaganda until April 1945. His opening words, 'Germany calling, Germany calling', delivered in an upper-class drawl, became a national catch phrase. At the beginning of the war he had more press attention than any BBC broadcaster. Soon thirty per cent of the nation was listening to him. This was the voice of the enemy speaking in your own home.

Joyce was born in the United States of Irish parents. As a child he lived in Ireland, but in 1922 his family emigrated to England. He came to Chelsea and a week after his twenty-first birthday married his first wife, Hazel, at Chelsea Registry Office. Joyce had piercing blue eyes, dishevelled hair and a deep scar disfigured his face. During a fight at a political meeting he was slashed with a razor across the cheek from mouth to ear. Usually he wore a shabby raincoat and scarf and carried a stick. In 1928 Joyce joined the Junior Imperial League

Prime Minister Harold Macmillan lived at 52 Cadogan Place
when young. In 1916 he arrived home gravely injured with
war wounds and his mother saved his life.

of the local Conservative Party and stayed two years. Some members were startled when he introduced military drill and stern discipline at meetings. At first his anti-Semitism was not apparent. Indeed his organizing skills and alleged working class background were admired. But others grew uneasy. When Joyce was discovered having an extra-marital affair he was forced to resign.

Joyce set up home at a number of Chelsea addresses including Number 77 Flood Street, a few doors from where Margaret Thatcher was later to live. The registers of electors for 1935 and 1936 reveal he had a flat at Number 37 Bramerton Street. The local library contains Joyce's application for a reader's ticket, signed by him and dated 2 November 1933. He gave his address then as Number 44 Jubilee Place, just off King's Road and his occupation as 'tutor'. Joyce was an unreliable borrower, however, and returned books late. An irate pencilled note written by a librarian says, 'Books returned without any fine paid. William Joyce must not borrow or be guarantor for anyone without first reporting above circumstances.'

In the same year he joined Sir Oswald Mosley's British Union of Fascists, but was expelled in 1937 for extremism. During this time he formed the Carlyle Club, which he named after the writer he admired who had lived close by. The club provided cover for political meetings and social gatherings.

Joyce spoke regularly at public meetings in Chelsea Town Hall, which was draped with black Fascist flags, but made little impact on British politics. The wife of a former mayor, Hester Marsden-Smedley, saw him one evening just before the war speaking from a rostrum in Sloane Square. Spurned by Britain he set off for Germany where he quickly gained international notoriety that led to his execution at the end of the war. In the 1930s he had obtained a British passport by claiming he was born in Ireland and this was his undoing. He was captured and tried as a traitor at the Old Bailey and hanged at Wandsworth jail in 1946.

As well as the traitor Joyce, spies have also trod the streets of Chelsea. The young Donald Maclean arrived in London in the mid-1930s, after coming down from Cambridge, and found a bachelor flat at Number 29 Oakley Street. 'He cut a distinctive figure striding through Chelsea in evening dress and black hat, with his silk-lined opera cloak swinging behind him,' wrote Andrew Boyle, who chronicled his misdeeds and those of the other Cambridge spies with whom he associated, Guy Burgess, Kim Philby and Anthony Blunt.

Maclean had just secured a post in the Foreign Office and there was talk of him one day becoming an ambassador. But appearances were deceptive. He was a committed Marxist, an alcoholic, had a violent temper and a scandalous private life. His colleague and fellow agent Guy Burgess had photographs of him in bed in the arms of another man.

Maclean served in Paris, Washington and Cairo as well as London and passed on to the USSR vital documents and decisions on nuclear planning. By 1951 he was a suspected traitor and fled to Moscow with Burgess. Their flight followed a tip-off from the so-called 'Third Man', Kim Philby, who warned they were about to be unmasked. Philby was the most successful of the Cambridge spies and arguably did more damage to Britain than any other spy. Between 1944 and 1951 he undermined the entire Western intelligence effort.

Philby had been a Communist since he was an undergraduate; at the beginning of the war he was recruited by the British Secret Service. Eventually this Soviet agent was put in charge of the anti-Soviet section of the Secret Intelligence Service (MI6). Later in Washington he liaised with the CIA. His career as a double agent took off in the mid-1940s and coincided with his arrival in Chelsea in 1944 with his mistress, Aileen Furse, and their three illegitimate children. They leased a large house at Number 18 Carlyle Square and Aileen set up a nursery school in the ground-floor dining-room, while a lodger helped pay the mortgage. Philby divorced his first wife (who was a Soviet spy) and on 25 September 1946 married Aileen who was expecting their fourth child. The wedding at Chelsea Registry Office was a quiet affair with only two witnesses, but they held a noisy party afterwards at Carlyle Square. Earlier in the year Philby was awarded an OBE for his war work.

The house was unruly and Aileen tolerated her husband's heavy drinking with good humour. Philby was a familiar figure round Chelsea, especially at the Markham Arms in King's Road where he appeared in corduroy trousers and a battered tweed jacket. He drove round London in an old taxi and looked like an eccentric don. No-one suspected that this diffident, charming man who stuttered, was a ruthless operator betraying hundreds of allied agents. In February 1947 he was posted to Turkey. He came under suspicion in 1951 when Burgess and Maclean vanished. Philby himself defected in 1963. When he died in 1988 he was praised by the official Soviet news agency, Tass, as the spy who was 'able to accomplish the impossible'.

KGB masterspy Kim Philby lived at 18 Carlyle Square with his mistress in the 1940s.

The radio traitor Lord Haw-Haw, who broadcast for Hitler, lived at various addresses in Chelsea including 37 Bramerton Street from 1935–6.

During the Second World War another secret agent, Greville Wynne, who was staunchly patriotic and anti-Communist, could be spotted entering a Queen Anne building on the Chelsea Embankment. Later he revealed in his memoirs that this was one of MI5's safe houses, a secret address where agents and people whose lives were in danger could live in strict security.

British intelligence contacted Wynne again in the mid-1950s and he used his business activities to cloak spying behind the Iron Curtain. Innocent businessmen and more sinister Soviet officials called at his Chelsea home, Number 19 Upper Cheyne Row, and one night he met a Soviet agent on a bench by Carlyle's statue down by the river. 'The evening was drizzly, the park deserted, the yellow lamplight a perfect atmospheric touch,' he wrote. Greville Wynne also frequented the Cross Keys pub nearby where he stopped off for a pint before dinner and a chat with the locals.

During his spying activities abroad he acquired the names and photographs of 300 enemy agents and discovered the Soviet leader Nikita Khrushchev had sent missile equipment to Cuba. With the aid of his links with the senior Soviet Intelligence officer Oleg Penkovsky, he was able to pass on a mass of military secrets to the West. Eventually the KGB caught up with him. He was arrested and imprisoned, but after eighteen months released in exchange for the Soviet spy Gordon Lonsdale.

When Wynne arrived home in April 1964 he was mobbed. Crowds of well-wishers and pressmen filled the road outside his Chelsea home. 'People rushed up to the car,' he recalled. 'I felt like a triumphant pop star.' And the landlord of the Cross Keys sent round a case of champagne. But Wynne's spying days were over and he became a property dealer abroad and died in 1990.

Spies and traitors may lead dramatic lives, but so do some politicians, none more so than Margaret Thatcher who was Britain's prime minister for eleven turbulent years. Before moving to Number 10 Downing Street she lived for twenty-five years in Chelsea, an anniversary that was celebrated by making her a freeman of the borough. At the age of 28 she married a wealthy managing director, Denis Thatcher, and they moved to a flat in Swan Court near King's Road. Later, in 1969, she and her husband bought a grey brick four-bedroom house at 19 Flood Street.

The Conservative Party was in opposition, but already as

their Shadow Cabinet spokesman on education Mrs Thatcher was a busy woman leaving home each morning at 7.30 to reach the House of Commons. The new colour scheme for her house was worked out in an hour. The hall was painted bright red and Mrs Thatcher struggled to fit in old furnishings with the new. 'We've been cutting down the curtains and carpets from our old London flat,' she said, 'and working out the best way of adding to the few bits of favourite Regency-style furniture that I'm keeping for the drawing-room.'

Mrs Thatcher was living there in 1975 when the Conservatives chose her as the first woman party leader in British politics. In the run-up to the 1979 general election when she became prime minister the press christened her 'The First Lady of Flood Street'. Sympathetic newspapers and magazines gave glimpses of her homelife in Chelsea. 'There are times when I get home at night,' she admitted, 'and everything has got on top of me, when I shed a few tears silently alone.' She told her interviewer she unwound by ironing and turning out the airing cupboard 'which I personally find very relaxing'. Newspapers portrayed her as a housewife superstar. Mrs Thatcher was the first British political leader to be photographed at the kitchen sink, rolling pastry and lifting a chicken out of the oven. A few weeks before the election Anne Edwards enthused in the *Sunday Express*: 'As I was talking to Mrs Thatcher a delicious smell of sizzling roast meat came floating up the stairs of her pretty, spick and span little house and this was just 9.30 in the morning ... '

Neighbours in Flood Street discovered advantages in having a prime minister at the end of the street. Never were they so well protected by police. 'Certainly keeps the burglars away,' remarked Admiral Porlock. Traffic jams vanished when a one-way system was introduced.

Mrs Thatcher lived in Chelsea for a month after she was elected prime minister, commuting each morning to Whitehall in a chaffeur-driven car. She soon moved into the flat at the top of 10 Downing Street, however, and eventually the house in Flood Street was sold. When the Thatchers bought their home in 1969 it cost them £28,000. In 1985 it was worth ten times that sum. Prospective buyers and visitors were surprised to find the house much as it was in 1979. There were security buzzers over the beds and Mrs Thatcher's pink rubber gloves still hung over the kitchen sink.

An innocent resting-place by day, but a spies' rendezvous by night. Here by Carlyle's statue in the embankment gardens, Cheyne Walk, Greville Wynne met a KGB agent.

View from the tower of Chelsea Old Church. In the distance Lots Road power-station. In the foreground Roper Garden laid out on the site of Whistler's, Epstein's and Laurence Olivier's studios which were destroyed by a bomb in 1941.

Houseboats near Battersea Bridge and Battersea Reach. On the right the World's End estate, in the centre Lots Road power-station, and up-river Chelsea Harbour which runs half a mile along the Thames.

11 Modern Times

Modern Chelsea dates from Bazalgette's construction of the embankment in the 1870s. Older houses along the river were replaced, notably by Norman Shaw, whose red brick Queen Anne style of architecture is seen to advantage in the Old Swan House and Clock House. In the north, around Cadogan Square, Shaw built more distinctive homes and in Pont Street other architects constructed Dutch style houses resembling those in Amsterdam.

Meanwhile at the end of the nineteenth century John Dando Sedding graced the southern end of Sloane Street with one of his best buildings, Holy Trinity Church. It replaced a smaller building by Savage and was regarded by Nikolaus Pevsner as 'the outstanding London example of the Arts and Crafts movement in the ecclesiastical field'. The nave is nine feet wider than St Paul's and the east window, designed by Burne-Jones, was the largest ever made by William Morris. Despite its architectural distinction, the building narrowly escaped destruction in the 1970s when there were plans to pull it down. John Betjeman, who worshipped there, and others campaigned for its preservation and the church was saved.

During the 1920s and 1930s blocks of flats went up in Chelsea and the striking department store, Peter Jones, was built in Sloane Square in 1936.

But war was on the horizon and during the bombing more than 500 people in Chelsea were killed. The Royal Hospital suffered damage and a bomb fell on Sloane Square station while two trains were waiting at the platforms. Some victims were never identified. The year 1941 saw the destruction of the Old Church and Epstein's and Whistler's studios in Cheyne Walk. On the night of 16 and 17 April 450 bombers swept over London. More than a thousand people died and over two thousand were seriously injured. Five parachute mines, high explosive bombs and hundreds of incendiaries fell in Chelsea. The Old Church dissolved in rubble, but miraculously the

Victorian lamp standard commemorating the opening of Bazalgette's Chelsea Embankment in 1874.

'What arches! What surprises!' exclaimed Norman Shaw when he set eyes on Sedding's masterpiece, Holy Trinity Church, Sloane Street – a celebration of the Arts and Crafts Movement.

Norman Shaw's Old Swan House, Chelsea Embankment – 'the pearl of his town house elevations'. Shaw won fame with his Queen Anne style architecture. Nearby is his Clock House.

More Chapel and most of the monuments were saved, and in the 1950s the church was rebuilt exactly as it was.

Many of the post-war buildings in Chelsea, especially those of the 1960s and 70s, are intrusive and out of place. The character of the area is under constant threat from developers and the view across the river to Battersea is marred by tall buildings.

The National Army Museum moved into a new building next to Wren's Royal Hospital in 1971. This preserves the history of the British soldier from Tudor times to the present. On show is the skeleton of Napoleon's charger, Marengo, captured at Waterloo in 1815 and the French Emperor's coffee urn. A vast model covering 420 square feet shows an aerial view of the battle. The model includes 75,000 minute figures a quarter of an inch high. The arms of the infantry move, drivers have whips in their hands and cannons, limbers and wagons have intricate details and wheels that revolve.

The museum also displays the order that sent the Light Brigade to destruction at Balaclava in 1854, the lamp Florence Nightingale was said to have carried in the Crimean War and General Gordon's magnifying glass. One of the world's largest collections of military uniforms is preserved here including clothes worn by Winston Churchill and the Duke of Windsor – a king's wardrobe. The Duke was colonel of forty-five regiments and amassed a large collection of orders and decorations, including the Danish Order of the Elephant.

A few minutes' walk from the army museum is the most extraordinary home in Chelsea. It is owned by the architect Richard Rogers, who designed the Pompidou Centre in Paris and Lloyds Building in London. He acquired two Regency houses in Royal Avenue and gutted them. The visitor steps through a Regency façade into a dramatic late twentieth-century interior, a vast cavern with stainless steel, polished wood, white walls and flying staircases. The two houses were knocked into one and a huge room two storeys high created, stretching from the first to third floor with a double set of windows. This living-room looks out on Burton's Court and Wren's Royal Hospital where the clock glows like a yellow moon at night.

Nearby in Glebe Place, the art dealer Martin Summers has created a roof garden on top of some former artists' studios. The garden, which has 800 potted plants, is decorated with four minarets from the Royal Pavilion, Brighton, from which emanate bird songs. The twitterings come from loudspeakers

Martin Summer's roof garden, Glebe Place. The minarets come from the Royal Pavilion, Brighton and contain loudspeakers that fill the air with birdsong.

Architect Richard Rogers poses in his vast living-room in Royal Avenue.

Chelsea Harbour fills a huge triangle of land each side of which is half a mile long. This self-contained city has an hotel, yacht marina, flats, restaurants, shops and medical services.

Lots Road was the world's largest power-station when built in 1904.
Designed by an American engineer it supplies electricity to the London
Underground and covers the site of the Cremorne Pleasure Gardens.

hidden inside. At the touch of a switch Mr Summers can fill the air with recorded woodland sounds, or the cry of seagulls. When darkness descends owls hoot and nightingales sing.

Far away in the north of Chelsea is another rooftop fantasy – the most expensive hotel suite in London. It costs £2,000 to stay one night in the Presidential Suite of the Hyatt Carlton Tower at Cadogan Place. From this eyrie eighteen floors up kings, presidents and wealthy business men can look down over the capital and on a clear day see as far as the South Downs. The German chancellor, Helmut Kohl, was once a guest. The suite is guarded by a barrage of security devices, including a steel door and a red panic button beside the master four-poster bed. A full-time butler and personal maid are on call.

At the far western end of the borough (strictly speaking beyond its boundaries in Fulham) lies a gleaming city of the future, Chelsea Harbour. 'I dreamed of building a great scheme on the bank of the Thames – a form which would respond to the great sweep on the river,' wrote the architect Ray Moxley. 'I wanted to build crescents, squares and avenues with slate roofs, gables and fine, glass domes. The composition would culminate in The Belvedere, a slender tower. A tower this far up river was a "must" for my dream – a tower with the yacht harbour at its feet and the great river coursing by on its way to the sea.'

Next door Lots Road power station belches smoke from its chimneys over the whole development. The scheme comprises apartments, town houses, shops, restaurants, landscaped gardens, an hotel and yacht marina. But despite the architect's dreams the effect is heavy and lifeless and upstaged by the electricity station.

None the less Chelsea Harbour appeals to the wealthy and the borough has flourished since the 1950s when King's Road was transformed from an ordinary thoroughfare with down-to-earth shops into a centre of fashion. It was there that Mary Quant set up her first boutique, Bazaar, and invented the miniskirt. Her husband Alexander Plunket-Greene created the first coffee bars. Their enterprise coincided with the revolution on stage at the Royal Court and the Chelsea Set made headlines. As King's Road rapidly changed into one of the most fashionable streets in London, property prices soared. On either side old Chelsea remains, but it is now the domain of the privileged. The ease and informality that existed until the 1960s have gone. The rich are under siege, their houses protected by multiple locks, barred windows, television cameras and alarms.

The less fashionable end of King's Road. Antique dealers have taken over ordinary Victorian shops. Chelsea Harbour and Lots Road power-station are nearby.

Chelsea modes.

Young lovers strolling along King's Road.

Tourists flock to the area and each year Chelsea becomes the focus of national attention when the Royal Horticultural Society stages its annual spring show in the gardens of the Royal Hospital. The flower show started in 1913 and was patronized from the beginning by the monarch and royal family. It is a five-day wonder where gardens and artificial landscapes, which look as if they have developed over decades, are created in a few days. Each year the world's largest marquee, covering three-and-a-half acres, sprawls over lawns, footpaths, football pitches and tennis courts.

A quarter of a million visitors come to the show, but occasionally discordant voices are heard. In 1983 there was the Great Gnome Controversy. There was an outcry when these little garden figures were banned. But the Director of the Victoria and Albert Museum, Roy Strong, complained, 'The banishment of gnomes is not enough.' The show was 'full of the most grotesque badly-cast figures and features that are, almost without exception, feeble reworkings from the past ... ' There was a crisis in garden design, he said, little colour sense and too much kitsch.

But, despite detractors, Chelsea Flower Show brings Ranelagh Gardens alive once more. The plants are exquisite and music from the Grenadier Guards wafts among the trees. It is a fantasy world of horticultural perfection, with tinkling water, artificial lakes, winding footpaths, fountains, arbours, shady dells and delicate scents. And this artificial world complements Chelsea itself – a square mile of delight where some of the most gifted, talented and unlikely people have come together over the centuries, and where the unexpected invariably happens.

And down by the Thames, despite encroaching buildings and roaring traffic, we may at twilight experience for a fleeting moment the atmosphere that once enraptured Whistler when 'the evening mist clothes the riverside with poetry as with a veil, and the poor buildings lose themselves in the dim sky, and the tall chimneys become campanili and the warehouses are palaces in the night and the whole city hangs in the heavens before us ...'

One of the marvels of the Chelsea Flower Show – an elaborate rock garden created in less than a fortnight.

Index

References in *italic* indicate illustrations.